FOOD, COOKERY
AND DIET

Food, cookery and diet

An information guide

Ray Prytherch
Suzanne Stanley

Gower

Aldershot · Brookfield USA · Hong Kong · Singapore · Sydney

Published by
Gower Publishing Company Limited
Gower House
Croft Road
Aldershot
Hants GU11 3HR
England

Gower Publishing Company
Old Post Road
Brookfield
Vermont 05036
USA

British Library Cataloguing in Publication Data

Prytherch, R.J. (Raymond John), *1945-*
  Food, cookery and diet: an information
  guide.
  1. Food science. Information sources
  I. Title II. Stanley, Suzanne
  641,1′07

Library of Congress Cataloging-in-Publication Data

Prytherch, Raymond John.
  Food, cookery, and diet: an information guide/Ray Prytherch.
  Suzanne Stanley.
      p.   cm.
  Includes index.
  ISBN 0-566-03568-5: £10.45 ($21.95) U.S.)
  1. Food — Bibliography. 2. Cookery — Bibliography.
  3. Nutrition — Bibliography. 4. Food service — Bibliography.
  I. Stanley, Suzanne. II. Title.
Z7914.F63P79 1989
(TX357)   88-24525
016.641 — dc19   CIP

ISBN 0 566 03568 5

Printed and bound in Great Britain by Anchor Press Ltd, Tiptree, Essex

Contents

Figures

Preface

An enormous quantity of material has been published about food; the literature covers the production of food, the processing of food, how it is to be prepared and cooked, and how its components affect the human metabolism.

This introductory volume examines the body of literature, organises it into main areas of interest, discusses a selection of important or representative titles, and explains how we can keep track of its ever growing quantity. Inevitably some items are omitted which it might have seemed advisable to include: these omissions may be due to limitation of scale − our desire not to allow what is intentionally brief to become too lengthy − or by a need to balance very popular areas of publishing against sparser topics. We have concentrated only on standard, basic sources, not on specialised needs; most of our material is in print and currently available at the time of writing, but items will become unavailable as time passes.

We should like to acknowledge the help given to us by friends and colleagues, especially Mandy Hicken of Derbyshire Library Service. We also appreciate the courtesy of James Askew and Son Ltd of Preston, Library Suppliers, in allowing us access to their showroom collection.

March 1988

RAY PRYTHERCH
SUZANNE STANLEY

Introduction

The concern of the consumer in the food we eat, the way it is prepared, and the information we have about its content, has grown throughout the 1980s. People have become much more aware of their health and the way in which their diet affects their well-being; concern is shown over methods of agricultural cultivation, animal welfare, and the activities of multinational food companies. This book is written to explain the many sources in which information is available — books, journals, videos — and the way in which indexing services help to organise information into a format in which we can quickly scan new materials for relevant items.

WHO ARE OUR READERS?

The intention of this volume is to assist anyone interested in food, diet, nutrition, cookery and hospitality management. Amateur cooks and chefs who are keen to learn more about the background to their hobby, and explore ways in which they can extend their knowledge and enjoyment will find many suggestions here. Professional caterers, restaurateurs, cooks and managers should be interested to see the range of material available, and to be reminded of the many publications and service organisations which offer support and advice. Students at all levels in the catering industry — craft, supervisory and management — will find this synopsis of the subject and the listing of standard information sources helpful.

Finally, we anticipate that librarians will use the book to assist in the development of their stock, both in range of coverage and in regard to selected titles of recent interest. School, college and public libraries will deal in some or all of the subject areas we cover, and this compendium will provide a convenient summary of the wide spread of topics.

COVERAGE

All aspects of the production, growing, rearing of the raw materials of food will be mentioned in this volume; the scientific background is briefly explored and sources for more extensive reading are listed. Food handling and processing and food technology are similarly treated. Nutritional concerns are included, especially the current interest in food additives and dietary requirements; food allergies; and special nutrition intakes for invalids, athletes and for the control of weight gain or loss. Methods of food preparation are discussed and exemplified in the range of current available recipe manuals.

ARRANGEMENT

Chapter 1 deals with the basic sources of reference: encyclopaedias, handbooks, histories, journals, articles and the means of tracing them. The scientific background is then examined, with academic and theoretical material grouped into categories. Chapter 3 deals with the needs of professional caterers — how to handle food safely and efficiently, managerial aspects, financial, legal and industrial topics. The education, training, and supervision of staff, careers open to catering students, and methods of self-employment with the industry are explored in Chapter 4.

The remaining two chapters examine and discuss the enormous range of recipe books available, dividing them into categories according to country or region, methods of cooking, ingredients, seasonal menus, speciality dishes; and special diets needed for medical conditions, weight problems and for general good health and fitness.

BIBLIOGRAPHIES

Comprehensive listings of cookery information are few, and most are of

North American origin and valuable principally for their historical coverage. Katherine Bitting's *Gastronomic bibliography* (California, privately printed, 1939) remains the great international source, covering 6000 items in several languages with some annotations. This, and Eleanor Lowenstein's *Bibliography of American cookery books 1742–1860* (American Antiquarian Society, 1972) are clearly only of historical value. Marguerite Patten's *Books for cooks* (Bowker, 1975) is an annotated bibliography of some 1700 cookery titles covering all types of cuisine and cookery, and now also somewhat dated. B. L. Feret's *Gastronomical and culinary literature* (Scarecrow Press, 1979) shows a heavy North American emphasis; and Syd Green's *Key guide to information sources in food science and technology* (Mansell, 1985) covers the scientific areas extensively, with a good bibliography.

CURRENT CONCERNS

The topics that are of immediate interest are well reflected in the literature; these are the items that show how food has become a popular subject for writers, and indicate the trends in public concern.

General good health through sensible and thoughtful eating habits are encouraged by E. Morse, J. Rivers and A. Heughan, *The family guide to food and health* (Barrie & Jenkins, 1988), which looks at nutritional needs of various age groups and the products of the modern food industry; Brian Ford's *Food book* (Hamish Hamilton, 1986) is a survey of what food does to us; and *Food in focus: a nutrition education programme for health educators*, edited by A. Carter and S. Bell (Wiley, 1988), is a package of programmes aimed at health workers to encourage them to specify healthy eating habits to their patients, based on the latest nutritional recommendations of the National Advisory Committee for Nutrition Education (NACNE) and the Committee on the Medical Aspects of Food Policy (COMA).

British food facts and figures (Woodhead Faulkner, annual) covers commodities, listed in alphabetical order, showing consumption, expenditure, source of supply, nutritional value, cooking and processing, and several related areas; the authoritative source of UK data. A similar title, *Food – facts and fallacies* by Allan Cameron (Faber, 1971), was an early attempt to examine the revolution in the production, processing and marketing of food, and highlighted health

3

problems that convenience foods and technological advances could involve. Geoffrey Cannon's *The politics of food: why the food industry doesn't want to listen to reason* (Century, 1987) examines the shortcomings of UK food policy; and John Walsh, *The meat machine: the inside story of the meat business* (Columbus, 1986), considers one aspect of the threat posed by multinational, multimillion pound industrial producers. Also by Geoffrey Cannon, with Caroline Walker, is *The food scandal: what's wrong with the British diet and how to set it right* (Century Arrow, 1986), which offers some unpalatable conclusions and was the subject of legal action.

Further concerns over food content are examined in our consideration of additives (Chapter 2) and other current problems are exemplified in such titles as *Food irradiation: the facts* by T. Webb and T. Lang (Thorsons, 1987).

Alternative lifestyles have something to say on cooking and eating; P. Bunyard and F. Morgan-Grenville, *The green alternative guide to good living* (Methuen, 1987), include material on environmental hazards posed by modern methods of agriculture, and examine health and nutrition. Alison Johnson's *Scarista style: a free range and humane approach to cooking and eating* (Gollancz, 1987) is a cookery book based on natural ingredients and strict avoidance of factory-farm produce and factory-reared animals.

For medical conditions, titles abound; James LeFanu's *Eat your heart out* (Macmillan, 1987) examines the nutritional arguments and queries the scientific base; later chapters here fully explore this area. Special diets are also necessary for athletes and other sports enthusiasts, and a typical title is *Staying flexible: the full range of motion,* Time-Life Fitness, Health and Nutrition Series (1988).

These concerns are legitimate and important, and are the means by which public concern has been developed and awareness enhanced. Needless to say, some material has been eccentric and bizarre; and one summary of the food craze is Anne Barr and Paul Levy, *Official foodie handbook* (Ebury Press, 1984), subtitled "Be modern, worship food", and examining in a very entertaining and informative manner leaders of style, the smart set, centres, pirates, journalists, ethnic influences, new fads, with sections on the history of foodism, the foodie lifecycle, global foodies and a who's who feature. This is an excellently designed and very funny satire on the "over-the-top" school of food enthusiasts.

ORGANISATIONS

Three major UK organisations feature prominently in certain sections of this book. The British Food Manufacturing Industries Research Association, always styled the Leatherhead Food RA, issues many vital publications which are discussed as reference materials and data for professional caterers; the Hotel and Catering Training Board (HCTB) is fully featured in Chapter 4 on careers, training and development.

The Hotel and Catering Industries Management Association (HCIMA) is the third principal organisation, and also appears in Chapter 4; the HCIMA annual *Reference book* is a membership directory and consists of some 500 large pages showing organisational activities, related groups, training and recruitment data; and has sections on management, technology, design, health, suppliers, vending machines and contract caterers. HCIMA is a very active body and its *Reference book* is an excellent introduction to the extent of its work.

1

Basic reference sources

Information on food, diet and nutrition is scattered throughout a range of many types of publications, and covers a range of subject areas — scientific, economic, social and educational. To trace basic information, simple factual data or standard recipes, a sound starting point is a good quality general encyclopaedia; more specific reference materials narrow down their subject coverage, and are supported by simple research sources, journals and classic cookbooks. Interesting insights can also be found in the history of food and cooking.

GENERAL ENCYCLOPAEDIAS

The standard encyclopaedias provide excellent coverage of many aspects of food, cooking, diet and nutrition; for basic information, facts and statistics, these sources are up to date, easy to use, and above all readily accessible in most libraries and many homes.

Encyclopaedia Britannica offers a very good range of material; the Micropaedia section which serves as an expanded index has articles on: food, new sources and products; quality control; the food chain; food poisoning; food preservation; food service systems; and food supply of the world. Each entry offers a brief summary and definition, lists the major articles in the Macropaedia section and, most vitally, lists the cross-references to all other places in the Macropaedia volumes in which related material can be found. In the section we have mentioned above some 140 cross-references are given to further relevant material; this Micropaedia/Macropaedia link, although initially cumbersome, is an excellent feature of *Britannica* and ensures maximum exploitation of all the articles. Similarly the Micropaedia entry for "Nutrition and diet, human", lists some fifty cross-references to other Macropaedia features apart from the main article on nutrition; these cross-references include bakery product enrichment; breast and bottle feeding; exercise energy requirements; food additives and quality control; salt uses and food-salting development; and vitamin intake. The precise reference to volume and page is cited in every instance.

The Macropaedia volumes of *Britannica* offer the fullest information on the topics; the article on "Food, new sources and products", runs to 5 pages well laid out with clear headings and sub-headings, tables, diagrams and a useful quick-reference key in the margins to permit rapid pin-pointing of relevant material. Each major article is followed by a valuable bibliography. The feature on nutrition and diet runs to 10 pages and extensive bibliography and covers the function of food, classes of food, recommended intake of nutrients, hunger and feeding behaviour, therapeutic diets, and public health nutrition. Other lengthy relevant articles appear elsewhere in the Macropaedia: protein and vitamin are terms treated at some length, for example.

The *Encyclopaedia Americana* has a similar single-alphabet format, and deals with food in a 12 page entry with illustrations and diagrams, covering world food supply – problems; needs; solutions; research; composition and sources of food – food from plants, animals and new sources; and the food industry. Cross-references are noted to many relevant headings such as bread; cattle; cheese; corn; meat; milk, and so on; and related articles deal with food additives; food preservation; canning; food poisoning; and frozen food. The article on nutrition runs to eleven pages, and *Americana* has an entry under cooking, which occupies eighteen pages and covers foods by type, equipment, methods and utensils; gives charts of cuts of meat; provides a glossary of terms, and is well illustrated.

Other commonly found general encyclopaedias would include *Collier's encyclopaedia* which treats food in a 14 page article in a good narrative, discursive style, divided clearly with subheadings, and followed by further pieces on food additives; flavours; poisoning; and cross-references to preservation techniques – canning industry; dehydrated and dried foods; and frozen foods.

Chambers encyclopaedia's article on food is brief, but notes other related headings to search – diet; minerals in nutrition; vitamins; digestion; and food types such as bread. Articles on food history; legislation; poisoning and preservation, follow the main piece.

Everyman's encyclopaedia has a main article under the heading "Food", with references to related topics – diet; famine; additives; minerals in food; nutrition; nutritional deficiency diseases; vegetarianism; and vitamins. Food control and food preservation are extensively treated with clearly written basic articles. Nutrition is also a featured heading, with a simple article, ideal as an introduction, but clearly needing to be supplemented if the standard and extent of the search warrants it.

Other encyclopaedias will also offer basic information on food, and can be a useful starting point for a factual query. Some however are not as regularly updated as those quoted, and the quantity and quality of their information will vary. Although general encyclopaedias are a useful beginning, and some like *Britannica* offer a great deal of information, more specialised sources can give a greater range of information, and in a more concise format.

SPECIALIST REFERENCE BOOKS

The spread of reference sources aimed at the cooking market contains both the very simple and the very comprehensive; our discussion will begin with the most basic materials and work towards some large-scale scholarly works. Sheila Bingham, *Everyman's companion to food and nutrition* (Dent, 1987), is a clear, up to date source that is simple to use, and reliable; it contains some 400 entries arranged in alphabetical order, and 250 nutritional analyses. Its coverage includes the history of food and cooking; content of common foodstuffs; information on chemical balance in food; the influence of certain foods on health and mood; details of food-affected medical conditions; and dietary considerations; as an introduction to the study of the topic it covers the ground well and is very clear in arrangement and layout. Carol Rinzler, *Food facts* (Bloomsbury Press, 1987), contains about 100 entries arranged alphabetically, being mainly entries relating to specific foods or food groups. Nutritional profiles are given, giving details of vitamin content, proteins, fats, calories, minerals, cholesterol and similar components.

The book also suggests nutritious methods of preparing and serving food, and covers diets; buying; storing and processing food; adverse effects associated with certain foods; and food/drug interactions.

Marc and Kim Millon's *Taste of Britain* (Webb & Bower, 1985) looks at regional cooking in the United Kingdom with historical notes and information on processes and methods in traditional use. Some recipes are included, but the book is also useful as a reference source for British cooking, with details of ingredients and food lore. It makes interesting reading through its attractive style and approach. Ruth Martin's *International dictionary of food and cooking* (Constable, 1973) is another basic guide, listing terms, food-names and processes in an alphabetical sequence. The layout is clear, concise and easy to use. Although definitions are very brief — sometimes only a single line — the coverage is excellent with close on 10 000 terms.

André Simon's *Concise encyclopaedia of gastronomy*, first published as a single volume in 1952 and reprinted repeatedly (Allen Lane, 1983), considers food types in various sections and is regarded as a classic standard source. By the same author, with Robin Howe, there is also the *Dictionary of gastronomy* (Nelson, 1970).

Patrick Coyle's *World encyclopaedia of food* (Facts on File, 1982) is a comprehensive source, listing some 4000 topics, mainly individual foods or food groups, and contains a bibliography and index. R. and D. de Sola's *Dictionary of cooking* (Constable, 1971) contains 9000 entries in alphabetical order covering culinary terms, methods, utensils and ingredients. T. Fitzgibbon, *Food of the western world* (Hutchinson, 1976), gives 6000 definitions and includes incidentally some 2500 recipes. It is well produced and contains tables showing cuts of meat and preparation methods.

On the more scholarly level, Robert Igoe's *Dictionary of food ingredients* (Van Nostrand Reinhold, 1983) discusses ingredients, listed alphabetically, defining functional properties and applications. The book divides into three sections: the first on ingredients includes chemical formulae, purpose and use, the second considers foods and components by categories — fats, flavours, flour, gums, spices, starch, vitamins, sweeteners, colours, antioxidants, emulsifiers, each group considered at some length — and a final section gives references to the sources quoted in the text.

On a larger scale there are three major encyclopaedias: Douglas and Glenn Considine's *Food and food production encyclopaedia* (Van

Nostrand Reinhold, 1982) runs to some 2600 pages covering all aspects of the science, engineering, technology, management and economics of food and the food industry; 1200 entries are included, with a good network of cross-references and an index of over 7500 terms. Major articles are supported by bibliographies, often from forty to sixty items. Coverage is international and begins with the growth and nurture of crops, animals and fish; followed by processing methods and processed food; diseases; chemicals; biochemistry and nutrition. Information throughout is comprehensive, and the book is a valuable tool for the specialist or for background on specific points for the general reader.

Secondly, the McGraw-Hill *Encyclopaedia of food, agriculture and nutrition* (1977), which is extracted from the publisher's major *Encyclopaedia of science and technology*, offers authoritative data assembled by numerous named contributors. The volume begins with a series of feature articles with titles such as "feeding the world", "energy in the food system", "foods from the sea", "the green revolution"; and then the main part of the work lists foods and processes in an alphabetical sequence supported in many cases by bibliographies. Many of the entries extend to several pages, for instance on food; vitamins; amino acids. An appendix shows the chemical composition of foods and the work concludes with a 22 page index; there are various tables, diagrams and monochrome illustrations.

The third major source is the *Encyclopaedia of food technology and food science*, issued in three volumes by AVI Publishing: I, *Encyclopaedia of food engineering* (1971); II, *Encyclopaedia of food technology* (1974); and III, *Encyclopaedia of food science* (1978). Each volume follows an alphabetical layout and entries are accompanied by numerous references.

JOURNALS

Journals, magazines and periodicals are an invaluable source of new information, innovative ideas, the latest developments and products, and up to date points on processes and methods. A variety of journals are published, ranging from the glossy and trendy to the dry and highly academic. General magazines, especially perhaps the traditional women's magazines, give regular space to cooking features and recipes, but cannot be covered here as their coverage is variable and often

10

simplified.

A key journal for those seriously interested is the *Caterer and Hotelkeeper* (Reed Business Publications; weekly) which contains copious news material, features, opinions, interviews, data on products, equipment, food lines, and letters. General and classified advertising pages offer product information and serving ideas, and obviously form the basis for professional job-seeking. Each issue is well illustrated, typically over 140 pages, and it is a vital weekly read for anyone with more than a passing interest.

Food and Cookery Review (Cookery and Food Association; bi-monthly) contains valuable reports and reviews, and a diary page. Trade and buyers' guides are a regular feature. *New Home Economics* (Forbes Publications; 10 issues per year) is a popular, highly readable magazine, well illustrated and also giving trade and buyers' information and a diary of shows, events and conferences.

British Food Journal (MCB Journals; bi-monthly) contains good feature articles and news of new developments. The American *Gourmet Today* (Cummins Publication; bi-monthly) offers information on products, people and events in a well-illustrated format. *British Hotel and Restaurateur* (British Hotel, Restaurant and Caterers' Association; monthly) gives organisational news, previews of events, reviews of products and services, and is well produced.

The technical side of the industry is represented by titles such as *Food Processing* (Techpress Publishing; monthly) which gives details of products, includes a buyers' guide and advertising, and a 'product-finder' feature using reply cards.

More scholarly periodicals cover food science, professional nutrition, hygiene and safety factors; titles include *Journal of Food and Nutrition* (Commonwealth Department of Health, and Dietitians' Association; quarterly), the *Journal of the Science of Food and Agriculture* (Elsevier Applied Science Publishers; quarterly) and *International Journal of Food Science and Technology* (Blackwell's Scientific Publications; bi-monthly); these are much more academic in approach and are relevant only to professional specialists in the food and catering industries.

Other readily available journals which will be of general interest are:

Catering (Dewberry Publications; monthly)
Food Production (Catalyst Publications; monthly)
Food Manufacture (Morgan Grampian; monthly)

Hospitality (HCIMA; monthly)
Nutrition and Food Science (Forbes Publications; monthly)
Popular Food Science (Reed Business Publications; 10 issues per year)

For market prices and sources of supply, the best regular journal is *The Grocer*, published weekly (William Reed Ltd). More specialised titles might include:

Bakers' Review (Turret Wheatland, for the National Association of Master Bakers, Confectioners and Caterers; monthly)
Meat Industry (Thomson Publishing; monthly)
Pizza and Pasta (Pizza and Pasta Association; quarterly)

RESEARCH MATERIALS AND ABSTRACTING SERVICES

The various aspects of food science and the food industry are inevitably the subject of academic and commercial research; many of the titles reviewed in Chapter 2 on the scientific study of food are based on lengthy research, or are papers collected and published after conferences or seminars. One regular series that deserves mention in the research context is the sequence of volumes of *Advances in food research* (Academic Press), which are scholarly in content, rich in references to further reading, and well indexed; recent volumes have dealt with topics such as smoking of meat; food texture; kiwi fruit; and baking quality of wheat flours (vol. 29, 1984); while volume 30 (1986) includes sections on sulphites in food; browning in food systems; fruit cells; soy sauce biochemistry; and new protein foods.

The sheer quantity of material published in such research reports, together with books on the subject and the large number of articles published each year in the scholarly and more popular journals and magazines, make it difficult for the serious student of food or the enthusiastic amateur cook or restaurant proprietor to keep track of all that is being done in the way of new cooking methods, developments in technology, improvements in food ingredients, new standards or legislation. To assist in keeping abreast of new publishing, there are a number of indexing and abstracting services that collect and summarise new books and journal articles.

Each of these tends to concentrate on one aspect of the topic, so that they complement each other and there is little duplication between the services available. The *Bibliography of hotel and catering management*, published quarterly by the Hotel Catering and Institutional Management Association (HCIMA), examines the contents of over eighty journals and divides the resulting abstracts into 150 subject sections. Each issue begins with a list of the journals scanned, with addresses and frequency; these are mainly of United Kingdom origin, but a small number are overseas — all are English language. Each article covered is arranged under an alphabetical subject heading, and the summary abstract of its content is well written (Figure 2.1); periodical citation is by code which is expanded in the initial list of journals. There is an extensive, clear index, and abundant cross-references (Figure 2.2); the index of each part in any year gives access to all other similar-topic articles earlier in the year, so that the cumulative index of the final part in each year is the starting point for searching through back files of the *Bibliography*.

Articles in hospitality and tourism is a monthly publication of Oxford Polytechnic Library and the University of Surrey Library; a brief section is devoted to tourism, but the larger part of each issue covers articles relating to the hospitality industry — hotels and catering. Articles are arranged by subject headings, which feature terms such as chefs; cook/chill; fast food; food presentation; hygiene; marketing; mobile catering; nutrition; and training. Headings are listed at the front of each issue and arranged in a full index at the end; some seventy journals are scanned, all English language but from a wide range including several general periodical titles that are the most difficult to keep track of. Each item cited is listed by title, author, abbreviated journal title and citation, and receives a running number comprising year, issue number and abstract number (for example 87/10/14); each summary abstract of content is brief but concise (Figure 2.3).

Food science and technology abstracts is issued monthly by the International Food Information Service (IFIS) and in addition to the paper copy is available as an online computer database; this service is international and is compiled with the help of organisations based in the UK, USA, West Germany, India and elsewhere. *FSTA* is divided into 20 sections which are listed on the back cover of each part, for example food science; hygiene and toxicology; food packaging; additives, and so on (Figure 2.4), and from 1987 onwards each of these sections is further subdivided; there are an author index and a subject index in each part,

EQUIPMENT:FOOD PREPARATION

'Fryers'
Carmen Konopka takes a close look at Deep Fat Fryers and offers advice to first time buyers.
PC Nov 87 p.43,45-47

'Frying tonight? give it thought'
Getting the right Fryer needs careful planning and a look at your individual operation. And a good Fryer deserves a good Oil too. Glenys Thomas
PUB 12 Nov 87 p.33,34

'Great Combinations'
Combination ovens incorporating Convection & Steaming.
CAT Oct 87 p.69-85

'Knight of the road'
Mobile Catering is moving up market. Oysters and Ethnic Snacks are served at Outdoor Events, while Mobile Kitchens provide midday meals for factory workers. Bruce Whitehall explains how to match the vehicle to the task.
CHK 24 Sep 87 p.80,81

'Living in a Vacuum'
Vacuum Packing is a simple process which can extend the shelf-life of food up to three, and sometimes five times longer than normal. Carmen Konopka
CHK 15 Oct 87 p.91

'Menu Boosters'
Bruce Whitehall looks at ways to attract custom with bright Displays, Lightboxes, Stickers, Mobiles and Panels.
CHK 5 Nov 87 p.83,85

'Planning for good value'
A growing variety of cooking Pans is available, as combinations of metals give the advantages of each without their disadvantages. Carmen Konopka
CHK 12 Oct 87 p.111,112

EQUIPMENT:FOOD SERVICE

'Knight of the road'
Mobile Catering is moving up market. Oysters and Ethnic Snacks are served at Outdoor Events, while Mobile Kitchens provide midday meals for factory workers. Bruce Whitehall explains how to match the vehicle to the task.
CHK 24 Sep 87 p.80,81

EQUIPMENT:TABLEWARE

'Style wise'
Are suppliers keeping up with needs and trends in the Tableware sector? London Restaurant Business asked the management of four different Restaurants about their choice of Tableware and suppliers. Anne Taylor
LRB 9 Nov 87 p.16-19

'The Designers set Beautiful Tables that mean business'
Too much emphasis is placed on saving money and not enough on using the tabletop as a Marketing tool. Candy L. Stoner
H&RI(USA) Oct 87 p.74-76,78,80

FAST FOOD

'Fast Food Formula'
Philip Ward finds some contrasting ideas at Pasta Mania and Southfork Fast Food outlets.
CHK (Interiors & Design) 15 Oct 87 p.XI,XIII

'Fast Food: Chain Events'
Its not just the meals that come rapidly in the Fast Food industry-so does change. Sue Meeson asks successful operators how they keep up the pace.
CHK 5 Nov 87 p.100,101,103

'French fashion a new Fast Food style'
Quick, cheap, but essentially stylish and up-market. James Burstall visited Oh! Poivrier!, an expanding French chain.
LRB 7 Dec 87 p.12,13

'Growth is the key to Williams' ambitions'
Home delivery in the UK and penetration of 45 European and Middle Eastern markets are among the plans for Pizza Hut. David Williams tells Mary Frayne about his strategy for PepsiCo.
PF Nov 87 p.35,36

'Higher profits fuel the C-Store push in the US'
Betsy Storm
PF Oct 87 p.18

'Petrie will build on Burgers and Pizzas'
UB Restaurants is to focus on sound growth in its two existing markets. Chief executive Ian Petrie discusses his strategy. Mary Frayne
PF Nov 87 p.39,41

'Pizza Hut'
Growth Management/Mismanagement. Frank Carney
CON(USA) Fall 87 p.67-74

'Spud bashers win Sales push'
A new look with more seating at Spud-U-Like Franchises aims to boost Sales and satisfy disgruntled operators. But Diana Campbell reports that there are still doubts.
CHK 15 Oct 87 p.19

'Takeaway delights'
Cookies and Croissants have become moneyspinners for two specialist chains. Ray Castle
PF Dec/Jan 88 p.38,40

'Centres of attention'
Sue Meeson examines the basic Themes for the future and finds that Food Courts rank high on the list with Drive Thrus and Home Delivery.
CHK 5 Nov 87 p.93,95,96

Figure 2.1 Bibliography of journals: subject headings with summary abstracts

Source: HCIMA bibliography, vol. 9, no. 1, January 1988.

Operating statistics, see
  finance
  food cost
  hotel and catering industry
  wages

Organisations, see
  hotel operators
  professional/trade organisations

Outdoor catering, see
  contract catering

Ovens, see
  equipment: food preparation
  microwave catering

Pensions, see
  conditions of employment

People: hotel and catering industry 18,

Personnel management: general 18,19,

Personnel management: hotel and catering industry 19,

Planning, see
  design and planning

Point of sale equipment, see
  computers
  equipment: electronic

Pork, see
  food commodities
  food preparation

Poultry, see
  food commodities
  food preparation

Premises, see
  design and planning
  property

Price display, see
  pricing

Pricing 19,
  see also
  menus

Prison catering 19,

Productivity, see
  personnel management
  training
  work study

Professional/trade organisations 19,20,
  see also
  HCIMA
  HCTB

Property 20,

Protein, see
  nutrition

Pub catering 20,

Public houses 20,

Publicity, see
  marketing: hotel and catering industry

Public relations

Purchasing 20,

Quality control, see
  management
  standards: hotel and catering industry

Racial discrimination, see
  discrimination
  legal: employment

Reception: front office 20,

Recipes, see
  food preparation: recipes

Recruitment, see careers

Reservation system, see
  computers
  equipment: electronic
  reception: front office

Restaurant design, see
  design and planning

Restaurant management, see
  management: hotel and catering industry
  restaurant operations

Restaurant operations 20,21,22,
  see also
  food service

Restaurant service, see
  food service
  liquor and beverage: service

Royal Air Force Catering, see
  armed forces catering

SCOTEC, see
  education

Safety, see
  fire
  health and safety

Salaries, see
  wages

Sanitation, see
  hygiene

School meals 22,

Security 22,

Self-catering accommodation, see
  hotel and catering industry

Service charges, see
  tipping
  pricing

Sex discrimination, see
  legal: employment
  women in hotel and catering industry

Figure 2.2   Bibliography of journals: extensive index with cross-references

Source: HCIMA bibliography, vol. 9, no. 1, January 1988.

15

Fast food

See   87/12/83

Food commodities

87/12/28 Focus on bacon
          GROCER 5 Dec.1987 59-118
                  A substantial feature on bacon as a food commodity

Food industry

See   87/12/73

87/12/29 Natural colours
          Side,C
          FOOD TRADE REV. 57(10) Oct.1987 541-542,544
                  A description of the way in which natural colours and
                  their properties differ from artificial ones, and of
                  those available for use in food

87/12/30 Future developments in the food industry
          Hawthorn,J
          J. ROYAL SOCIETY HEALTH 107(6) Dec.1987 215-217
                  There are many new developments in food science
                  with implications for the food industry. Such
                  developments are often very slow to be recognized and
                  and accepted however

Health foods

87/12/31 Is food "education" a waste of time?
          Salmon,J
          FOOD MANUFACT. 62(12) Dec.1987 39-40
                  Attitudes towards diets have changed only
                  slightly during the past five years in spite
                  of the extensive media coverage given to
                  ..ealth foods

Hospital catering

87/12/32 Putting cook-chill into perspective
          Jenner,G
          CATER. HOTELKEEP. 178(3500) 3 Dec.1987 17
                  A report of the Hospital Caterers Association's
                  national symposium on cook-chill

87/12/33 Cost-cutting surgery
          Ivory,M
          CATER. HOTELKEEP. 178(3500) 3 Dec.1987 48-49
                  Cost saving exercises made by the Queen's Medical
                  Centre, Nottingham. These include contract
                  catering for another hospital using cook-chill
                  facility, using agency workers at basic rates
                  during busy periods and publicising the staff
                  restaurant for use by hospital visitors

**Figure 2.3   Articles relating to the hospitality industry: concise
summary abstracts**

Source: Articles in hospitality and tourism, monthly.

16

Abstract Sections

A Basic food science (chemistry, physics, biochemistry, biophysics)

B Food microbiology

C Food hygiene and toxicology

D General-Food economics and statistics

E Food engineering (equipment and processes)

F Food packaging (materials and methods)

G Commodity technologies-General (including papers on several commodities and on prepared, synthetic, dietary foods, etc.)

H Alcoholic and non-alcoholic beverages

J Fruits, vegetables and nuts

K Cocoa and chocolate products

L Sugars, syrups, starches and candy

M Cereals and bakery products

N Fats, oils and margarine

P Milk and dairy products (including butter)

Q Eggs and egg products

R Fish and marine products

S Meat, poultry and game

T Food additives, spices and condiments

U Standards, laws and regulations

V Patent literature

Author Index

Subject Index

Figure 2.4 Abstracts of food science and technology: list of contents

Source: Food science and technology abstracts, monthly.

Figure 2.5   Abstracts of food science and technology: subject index

Source: FSTA, vol. 19, no. 12, 1987.

in stalks of N:CO in October. Optimum harvest time of Chikusha sugar cane was considered to be in October due to its high sugar and cis-aconitic acid contents which eventually affect sensory quality of sugar.   EL

12 L 5
Effect of nitrogen fertilization on yield and quality of sugarbeet.
Kapur, M. L.; Kanwar, R. S.
Indian Journal of Agricultural Sciences **57** (5) 336-342 (1987) [16 ref. En] [Punjab Agric. Univ., Sugarcane Res. Sta., Jalandhar, Punjab 144 001, India]

3 sugarbeet (*Beta vulgaris*) cv., i.e. Ramonskaya 06, Automonosoras, and JISR Comp. I, were used for a 2-yr field experiment in which 5 levels of N fertilization were applied (0, 50, 100, 150 and 200 kg ha^{-1}). Parameters evaluated included sucrose concn. in roots, which decreased as N level increased. Sucrose % in the 3 cv. were 14.6-16.2, 14.4-15.7 and 14.2-15.9, resp., over the 2 yr.   LJW

12 L 6
A new continuous evapor-crystallization tower for white sugar and low raw products.
Bosse, E. D.
Sugar y Azucar **81** (5) 33, 36-37, 40, 42, 46, 48, 50, 53, 56 (1986) [7 ref. En] [Braunschweigische Maschinenbauanstalt, A.G., Braunschweig, Federal Republic o' Germany]

After introducing developments in the field of evapocrystallization (EC), principles of continuous EC tower operation are detailed and illustrated. Design parameters are referred to, heat economy and seeding is calculated, the boil-out system is described, and the Chamber-Wise cleaning cycle is illustrated. Chamber-Wise cleaning and intermediate massecuite storage are discussed and some results obtained using a continuous pan are detailed. Technological aspects of an EC system are outlined, e.g. uniform use of heat, and construction requirements are briefly referred to.   EL

12 L 7
[Ammonium and calcium bisulphites in diffusion.]
Vaccari, G.; Mantovani, G.; Velentza, I.; Sgualdino, G.; Maurandi, V.; Turtura, G.; Zani, G. C.
Alimentacion Equipos y Tecnologia **5** (3) 48-56 (1986) [6 ref. Es] [School of Sugar studies, Univ. de Ferrara, Ferrara, Italy]

The use of ammonium and calcium bisulphites in a sugar-refining process is described. The function of the salts as auxiliary agents during the pressing of the pulp, their effect on the quality of the juice, as well as the effect of SO$_2$ (as ammonium bisulphite) on bacterial growth in juices stored in an anaerobic-diffuser, are detailed in a series of experiments. The studies and their results are summarized diagramatically, together with those obtained (under different conditions) for the previous session. Simultaneous addition of calcium bisulphite at the tail-end of the diffusers, and ammonium bisulphite at the head-end, to slices of sugar-beet transported by conveyor belt, is reported to ensure practically total sterility in the juices and in the diffusers, thus circumventing the need for disinfectants normally required (i.e. formaldehyde, carbamates). Under those conditions, the thick juice obtained after pressing was only slightly coloured and the need for SO$_2$ in the diluted juices (as decolorant) was reduced.

No traces of SO$_2$ were found in the final sugar. An increase in DM content is reported for the pulps after the pressing stage, due largely to precipitated sulphates. Laboratory studies on the effect of SO$_2$ levels on the bacterial population normally present in juices from diffusers operating under anaerobic conditions indicated that SO$_2$ acts as a bacteriostatic agent. Different SO$_2$ levels were needed for aerobic- and anaerobic-bacteria (200 p.p.m. and 400 p.p.m., resp.). Some of the economical advantages obtained by use of SO$_2$ compared with use of H$_2$SO$_4$ plus disinfectants are outlined.   MN

12 L 8
[Effects of attack by *Sesamia nonagrioides* (Lepidoptera; Noctuidae) on technological quality of sugar cane.]
Hilal, A.
Actes de l'Institut Agronomique et Veterinaire Hassan II **5** (1/2) 37-42 (1985) [7 ref. Fr, ar, en] [INRA, Cent. de Recherches Agron, Beni-Mellal, Morocco]

12 L 9
Clarification of sorghum juice for syrup by using bentonite and heat.
Collins, J. L.; Ebah, C. B.; McGarty, I. E.; Mount, J. R.
Tennessee Farm and Home Science No. 142, 16-20 (1987) [5 ref. En] [Dep. Food Tech. & Sci., Univ. Tennessee, Knoxville, Tennese, USA]

The effects of bentonite and heat to remove solid particles from sorghum syrup thus improving quality were investigated. 125 pounds of bentonite and diatomite/1000 gal juice were used to filter juice which was heated for 5 min. °Brix, pH, total acidity, lightness-darkness, and flavour of the clarified juice were evaluated after 4 months storage. Results are tabulated, showing an average °Brix of 79.3-82.5, with pH ranging from 4.8 to 5.0, total acidity from 0.49 to 0.66% and lightness-darkness scores of 3.3-35.3. The treatments affected juice appearance and lightness of the resultant syrup but did not affect other quality attributes studied.   EL

12 L 10
[Chromatographic and spectrophotometric study of molasses composition.]
Gulyuk, N. G.
Sakharnaya Promyshlennost' No. 10, 23-25 (1986) [2 ref. Ru] [NFO po Krakhmaloproduktam, USSR]

Molasses composition was studied by liquid chromatography followed by spectrophotometry of individual fractions. Biogel R-2, characterized by a high selectivity was used. Samples of molasses from various harvests and sugar beet growing regions were used. At least 8 fractions were observed, of which 3 were detected in the visible region and the others absorbed light in the UV region. The characteristic spectral curves of individual fractions and their elution rates were also determined. The most intense colour was in the highest mol wt. fraction, and accounted for >66% of molasses colour.   STI

12 L 11
[Dispersivity of pigments in raw sugar and sugar products.]
Bobrovnik, L. D.; Sheiko, G. I.; Dubinina, N. V.; Oleinik, A. V.

Figure 2.6   Abstracts of food science and technology: full informative summary

Source: FSTA, vol. 19, no 12, 1987.

printed on coloured paper (Figure 2.5), and each year a separate annual index volume is issued. Access via the online service is faster and more up to date than dependence on the printed copies.

The summary abstracts are numbered by issue, section and running number, and include an English title in bold print, a note of the original title for non-English works, details of authors, editors, citation, a note of the number of references included, address of the main author, and a full informative summary of content (Figure 2.6). Each abstract is initialled by its compiler. This is the largest scale international source in the subject, invaluable to scholars but perhaps too extensive for rapid occasional use.

Also of value for some of its content is series A (Human and Experimental) of *Nutrition abstracts and reviews*, issued monthly by the CAB International Bureau of Nutrition, Aberdeen. This carries good abstracts within its field, and useful summary review articles, with very copious references; an important scholarly source.

The Leatherhead Food Research Association provides many services to its members that are relevant to this chapter; the chief of these is the Food RA Online Scientific and Technical Information database (FROSTI) which has been assembled since 1975 and now contains 150 000 references to books, journal articles, conference papers and patent specifications. Most items are summarised in a brief abstract, and the area of coverage embraces all important aspects of the subject.

Members can also benefit from the Food Scanning database (FOSCAN) which issues daily a briefing on items in United Kingdom media sources including health, government activity, EEC news and company news. A weekly printed summary is also prepared.

On a smaller scale a monthly Abstract Journal is produced containing new material entering FROSTI; a current awareness bulletin on *Food topics*, which is issued every two months, lists recent references to a wide range of subjects. *Food patents* summarises new UK and foreign patent application. In support of these services, the Leatherhead Food RA operates databases of its periodical holdings (750 titles) and its library book stock (7000 items).

REFERENCE COOKBOOKS

No section on culinary reference sources could neglect the value of classic cookbooks; some of the great names are encyclopaedic in their coverage and are an essential initial source on recipes, ingredients and methods. Isabella Beeton's *Book of household management* (1861; reproduced in facsimile, Jonathan Cape, 1968) must be one of the most famous cookbooks ever; entertaining from a culinary and social viewpoint, the recipes are classics of overindulgence to modern taste. Mrs Beeton died at the age of twenty-eight; her husband was a publisher and issued the book – but he met with catastrophic financial ruin.

Auguste Escoffier is the second great name; his *Guide to modern cookery* (1907; 2nd edn, Heinemann, 1957) is from the French edition of 1902 and contains almost 3000 recipes, divided into a section on fundamentals – sauces, jellies, garnishes, routine operations, and so on – and then by type of food, with sample menus. Perhaps more for chefs than home cooks, but a masterly book; an excellent index is provided. Escoffier's other work, *Ma cuisine* (Flammarion, 1934), is also available in an English version by Vyvyan Holland, edited by Marion Howells (Hamlyn, 1965 and subsequent reprints).

The essential reference cookbook must be *New Larousse gastronomique*, "the world's greatest cookery reference book" (Hamlyn, 1977, based on a French text of 1968). Originally published in France in 1938 this is an alphabetical encyclopaedia of food edited by Prosper Montagné, and covering history, principles, methods of preparation, origins of ingredients; and featuring some 8500 recipes. Articles range from two-line definitions to entries of several pages; there are extensive cross references and an excellent index of over 55 pages.

Other great standard cookbooks include the two-volume *Gourmet cookbook* (Gourmet Corporation/Hamish Hamilton, 1950 and 1957) with a total of over 4000 recipes and a good index to each volume, but unfortunately not a combined index to the two volumes; and the *Robert Carrier cookbook* (Nelson, 1965), beautifully clear and easy to read, with excellent introductory sections on the art of eating, the enjoyable kitchen and similar topics, and chapters then divided by type of food. André Simon's *Concise encyclopaedia of gastronomy* has been mentioned previously, but could feature here again for its large number of recipes.

At a much more basic level the "standard" guides would include the Good Housekeeping Institute's *Good Housekeeping cookery book* (Ebury Press, 1976), which covers all the basics of culinary technique, is well produced and well indexed. For United Kingdom recipes, the key source could be Lizzie Boyd's *British cooking: a complete guide to culinary practice in the British Isles* (Croom Helm, 1976); this publication was sponsored by the British Tourist Authority and the British Farm Produce Council, and considers 2000 native recipes from all parts of the British Isles. Introductory sections examine the background to regional cookery, its history and traditional methods; and the recipes are followed by a bibliography and index.

HISTORIES

Interesting sidelong glances at the history of food, cooking and eating can enhance our understanding and appreciation of modern practices. A number of standard works have been published; most show the social changes that have been mirrored in our eating habits.

Reay Tannahill's *Food in history* (Eyre Methuen, 1973) takes as its theme the idea that food *is* history, and draws on archaeology, anthropology, biology, ecology, zoology, technology and economics to collect evidence to support this. Sections begin with the prehistoric period, then the ancient Near East, Egypt, classical lands, Asia and Arabia; Europe is covered in two sections AD 1000–1500, and AD 1500–1800, followed by the "New World". The industrial revolution, the food and supply revolution, and the scientific revolution are each examined, and the book carries an extensive bibliography and index. Illustrations are a useful complement to the text.

Jean-François Revel's *Culture and cuisine* (Doubleday, 1982; translated from the French edition, 1979) is described as a journey through the history of food, and covers all ages and all countries. Chapters cover such topics as sources of cuisine, bread and wine, medieval period, and international cooking. Illustrations are good, and there is an adequate index.

The classic history of British cooking is Dorothy Hartley's *Food in England* (Macdonald, 1953, variously reprinted) which has 27 chapters covering all manner of topics — kitchens, fuels and fireplaces; poultry and game; feast and famine; trade, magic and religion; salting, drying and preserving; the sailors' cook; house and garden in 1600; coaching days; and the industrial revolution. Although this makes fascinating reading it is biased towards the rural life and is a little idiosyncratic; drawings in the text are valuable, and many recipes are quoted in passing. Index and bibliography are useful although neither is well assembled.

Christopher Driver's *The British at table 1940–1980* (Chatto and Windus, 1983) is entertainingly written and covers a period of profound social change – the disappearance of servants; foreign influences; industrialisation; wartime to affluence; and the arrival of food writers. The first part of the book examines the history of the period "from lean to fat", and the second treats various themes on why we eat as we do: the "melting pot" of tastes; additives; quality; chefs. The bibliography covers useful additional reading.

C. Anne Wilson's *Food and drink in Britain: from the Stone Age to recent times* (Constable, 1973) examines the topic by types of food: thus sections cover game hearts and tame hearts; fish and salt; cereals, potherbs and pottage, for example. There are plenty of references throughout and a long bibliography. Also valuable for its historical content is Drummond and Wilbraham's *The Englishman's food* (Cape, 1964 reprint).

ON A LIGHTER NOTE

Food and cooking bring out the best in many people; the delights of eating have fascinated many authors and now a number of anthologies and anecdotes have been published, bringing to light stories and themes that will delight anyone who takes pleasure in this topic. Serious cooks and serious diners may not seek strictly factual information in these volumes, but their background reading will be painlessly enhanced; the range of facts, stories, recipes and travellers' tales bring many fresh insights for the food enthusiast.

Alexandre Dumas, père (author of *The Three Musketeers*) compiled a *Grand dictionnaire de cuisine* in 1870, nearly three-quarters of a million words in length, and fascinating in parts, though monumentally dull in others; the English translation by Alan and Jane Davidson, *Dumas on food* (Michael Joseph, 1979), collects the best of the work.

Feasts: an anthology (Constable, 1987) collected by Christopher Bland and Linda Kelly, concentrates on meals described in literature. The main period is the nineteenth and early twentieth century, but some earlier treatments are included. Maria Robbins's *Cook's quotation book* (Hale, 1987) records the writings and sayings on cooking and drinking of many famous figures, from Samuel Johnson to Miss Piggy, and including James Joyce and Graham Greene on the way.

"Literary" figures who have collected essays on food are numerous; some such collections become precious and tedious but, for the enthusiast, a few can be rewarding. Paul Levy's *Out to lunch* (Chatto and Windus, 1986), contains sixty pieces ranging over all sorts of cooking all over the world and is an entertaining read. Clement Freud, *No one else has complained* (Elm Tree Press, 1987), explores the battlefield between restaurateur and customer and reports humorously on the etiquette of the encounter. Excesses are the subject of Charles Gattey's book, *Excess in food, drink, sex* (Harrap, 1986), with "colourful" examples; while Simon Loftus writes *A pike in the basement: tales of a hungry traveller* (Century, 1987), a very rewarding "travel book with recipes".

Splendid recipe books owing more to style than to the sheer basic culinary information include Elizabeth Luard's *The princess and the pheasant and other recipes* (Bantam, 1987), an illustrated collection of recipes first appearing in *The Field*; and Digby Anderson's *Spectator book of imperative cooking* (Harrap, 1987), based on his *Spectator* columns, emphasises the need for discipline in the kitchen.

Of some entertainment value also are collections of recipes mingled with anecdotes from the pen of celebrities. Quality varies but here again enthusiasts may find amazing facts and valuable hints. Recent titles of this type include Elizabeth Jane Howard and Fay Maschler's *Howard and Maschler on food* (Michael Joseph, 1987) with 20 chapters reflecting occasions, such as the winter picnic, the seductive meal or the house-warming supper. Jane Grigson's *Food with the famous* (Michael Joseph, 1979) re-examines novels, pictures and houses to pick at their culinary mentions: John Evelyn, Jane Austen, Monet and Proust are among those selected.

Beryl Reid's *Beryl: food and friends* (Ebury Press, 1987), contains recipes and anecdotes; buying from markets and shared meals with famous friends are the key features. The *House of Commons cookery book*, compiled by C. Irving (Century, 1987), contains 150 favourite recipes from luxurious to snacks, divided into types of dish, and featuring contributions from MPs of all parties.

The lighter side of reference material is perhaps a contradiction in terms, but many of these suggestions contain excellent material, and make profitable browsing.

2

The scientific background

The levels of the scientific study of food and cooking are complex; the general reader may be concerned to find a discursive synthesis of current research, while students of catering will need thorough and detailed basic texts, and the academic researcher will require scholarly material reflecting the latest progress. The most academic studies of food and cooking are probably of interest only to a small number of specialists and are too complex for the lay person; those whose interests lie in this direction will already be aware of their sources, and this volume deliberately makes no attempt at a discussion of high-level texts. Instead we shall consider the basic textbooks that are of value to the student and the amateur. There are a number of good standard titles.

GENERAL WORKS

Eva Medved's *Food in theory and practice* (Plycon Press, 1978) remains a useful introduction; its first section deals with the basics of scientific study — the nature of food and the foundations for food preparation — and the second part is concerned with the principles of preparation, discussed by type of food and examining composition; nutrient content; processing; safety; storage; packaging methods and additives. The third section of the book explores the management of food science, covering cooking systems; preservation methods; consumer protection; and similar topics. There are valuable summaries and bibliographies with each chapter, and several appendices.

Marion Bennion, *Introductory foods* (8th edn, Collier Macmillan, 1985), is a popular basic text first issued in 1940; it covers food composition; safety and quality; nutrition; preparation; cookery of various food types; and fuller chapters offer information on fats, sugar, starches and related aspects. Clearly laid out, with summary tables and glossary, the volume also features high quality colour illustrations.

George Stewart and Maynard Amerine's *Introduction to food science and technology* (2nd edn, Academic Press, 1982) also covers the basic ground and has useful sections on sensory properties of foods; shelf life; law and regulations; and health issues. Brian Fox and Allan Cameron's *Food science: a chemical approach* (4th edn, Hodder & Stoughton, 1982) examines enzymes, alcohols and acids, amino acids and proteins, vitamins, carbohydrates, and aspects of food hygiene and preservation.

R. K. Proudlove, *Science and technology of foods* (Forbes Publications, 1985), takes a sensible and concise look at the composition of foods; how the composition can be applied in studying commodities and raw materials; processes and the changes that occur in cooking; and preservation and packaging technology; a thorough review with clear diagrams. John Hawthorn's *Foundations of food science* (W. H. Freeman, 1981) is also a useful basic text, giving essential data in a straightforward format.

Magnus Pyke's *Food science and technology* (4th edn, John Murray, 1981) is a well written and popular account, and none the less accurate for its attractive style; it considers scientific principles as applied to food; practical technology; animal growth; fish curing; composition of milk; chemistry of cheesemaking; and other pragmatically written chapters. Harold McGee, *On food and cooking: the science and lore of the kitchen* (Allen & Unwin, 1986), is a lighter treatment, enlivened with history and anecdote, examining food by type; food and body; and the principles of cooking. It is well illustrated and easily understood.

Two older guides which remain in circulation and are still popular are Margaret McWilliam, *Food fundamentals* (3rd edn, Wiley/Macmillan, 1979); and F. E. Deatherage, *Food for life* (Plenum Press, 1975), which combines scientific information with social and economic concerns of food supply, and notes cultural forces that affect the production, processing, distribution and consumption of food.

Recent student texts that are accessible for the general reader also include the *Dictionary of nutrition and food technology* (5th edn,

Butterworth, 1982); A. G. Cameron, *Science of food and cooking* (3rd edn, E. J. Arnold, 1985), which is well illustrated and includes "activity" sections; and V. L. Brownsell, C. J. Griffiths and E. Jones, *Basic science for food studies* (Longman, 1985).

P. M. Gaman and K. B. Sherrington, *Science of food* (2nd edn, Pergamon, 1981), is written for the catering trade, and is a simplified, but valuable summary; Ray Hopwood's two volumes, *Elementary food science* and *Advanced food science* (G. Bell, 1975), are aimed at specific trade examinations. Also reliable and popular are G. V. Robins, *Food science in catering* (Heinemann, 1980); and O. F. G. Kilgour, *Complete catering science* (Heinemann, 1986).

FOOD TYPES

To supplement the general and comprehensive texts mentioned above, the reader should also be aware that detailed scientific and technological material is available for each of the main categories of food. To the student and enthusiastic general reader such works are not difficult to understand and provide information in a format more concise and specific than the general textbooks.

Examples of these publications include N. L. Kent's *Technology of cereals* (3rd edn, Pergamon, 1983), which deals with crops, structure, chemical composition, cleaning, milling, nutritional aspects, baking technology and processing; individual types are also examined in more detail − wheat, barley, oats, rye, maize, rice and millet − and the book contains a bibliography. Albert Daniel, *Bakery materials and methods* (4th edn, Applied Science Publishers, 1963, reprinted 1978), considers all aspects of breadmaking − fancy and plain; the faults that arise; nutritional aspects; and equipment; confectionery is then explored including flours, fats and oils; sugars, fruits and nuts; colours and flavours; pastry, meringues and so on; with a note on costings. S. A. Matz's *Ingredients for bakers* (Ellis Horwood, 1987) surveys all the technological points concerned with bakery ingredients including composition and nutritional components.

The standard classic on meat is Frank Gerrard, *Meat technology* (5th edn, Northwood Publications, 1977 and MTJ Books, 1978), which examines growth, breeds, slaughter, dressing, quality, preservation, cutting and packing. A glossary of EEC terms is included. R. A. Lawrie, *Meat science* (4th edn, Pergamon, 1985), deals with similar information including the chemical and biochemical constitution of meat.

William Stadelman and Owen Cotterill's *Egg science and technology* (3rd edn, AVI, 1986) devotes chapters to the egg industry; production practices; identification of structure; regulations; sizing; preservation; nutritional value; merchandising; freezing; and quality control. There are appended sections on patents; and related readings.

Lincoln Lampert, *Modern dairy products* (3rd edn, Chemical Publishing, 1975), thoroughly examines composition; food value; processing; chemistry; bacteriology; testing; substitutes are considered product by product. *Sugar: science and technology,* edited by G. G. Birch and K. J. Parker (Applied Science Publishers, 1979), consists of a series of papers which deal with the history of sugar; economics; refining techniques; colour; chemistry; technology; quality; storage; analysis, dietary effects; and dental caries.

FOOD PREPARATION

The theoretical background to the preparation of food is the subject of many books; obviously the recipe books discussed elsewhere are summaries of preparation methods for specific dishes, but the underlying methods are exhaustively dealt with, and this can be valuable to students, mass caterers and amateurs keen to understand more of *why* cooking works in addition to *how.*

Donald Lundberg and Lendal Kotschevar's *Understanding cooking,* edited by Victor Ceserani (Edward Arnold, 1970, reprinted subsequently) is a student guide in question and answer format — answers are printed in the margin so that they can be readily concealed; revision summaries are given for each section. The layout and organisation of the book is very clear, and sections cover the cooking process; sauce cookery; soups; egg cookery; fish and shellfish; the frying process; meat cookery; poultry and game; salads; vegetables; baker's products; notes are added on starch, control of crystallisation; and a glossary of terms. Clive Finch's *Food preparation* (Pitman, 1987) is designed to be used with BTEC, HCIMA and City and Guilds courses, but it is also very useful for general reference purposes. Topics are arranged by type of food with several helpful tables, a glossary, list of abbreviations and a storage summary. Several recipes are included and these have assessment notes, explanations of problems, causes and solutions.

Gladys Peckham and Jeanne Freeland-Graves, *Foundations of food preparation* (4th edn, Collier Macmillan, 1979), is a thorough guide to the subject; science and food are discussed; the purposes of cooking; physical and chemical properties; and microbiological aspects. Economic points, evaluation, management principles and kitchen planning are also introduced. The main section of the book deals with foods by type, and there are chapters on preservation; food controls — standards and regulations; and a glossary of terms, weights, measures and nutrients in domestic quantities. Daniel Stevenson's *Professional cookery: the process approach* (Hutchinson, 1985) has a substantial introduction consisting of "key information" (methods, principles, technology, food handling), then a "complete reference guide", which is an expanded contents page and index with menu lists, culinary terms, fundamental procedures and commodity preparation. A series of sections then deal with such topics as cold preparatory work; boiling and poaching; steaming; roux thickening; amd microwave cookery. Each section ends with an assessment exercise — a series of questions to show understanding, and essential activities — a flow-chart style summary of the section's main points.

FOOD PROCESSING

The processing of food in mass catering and industrial settings is the subject of H. Muller and G. Tobin's *Nutrition and food processing* (Croom Helm, 1980), which examines the chemistry of nutrition; the evaluation of nutrients; proteins; various foods arranged by type; refining additives; refrigeration, heating and dehydration; and diseases that can arise in processing. Dennis Heldman and Paul Singh's *Food process engineering* (AVI, 1983) considers the processes and equipment involved: rheology; heating and cooling; evaporation; and separation are among the topics covered.

NUTRITION AND ANALYSIS

Standard sources for data on the nutritional values of food include the Ministry of Agriculture, Fisheries and Food (MAFF), *Manual of nutrition* (9th edn, HMSO, 1985), and the Food and Agriculture Organisation (FAO), *Food composition tables* (HMSO, 1976). Other major published standard sources include R. McCance and E. Widdowson, *Composition of foods* (4th edn compiled by A. A. Paul and D. A. T. Southgate, Medical Research Council, HMSO, 1978), with supplements issued in 1980, and 1985; and S. Bingham, *Dictionary of nutrition* (Barrie & Jenkins, 1977). *Pearson's chemical analysis of foods* (8th edn revised, Churchill Livingstone, 1987), first published in 1926, is a very full treatment of methods and food content, and has a number of useful appendices listing organisations issuing standard analytical methods; EEC directives and regulations; regulations applicable in the UK for composition and labelling; additives and contaminants; and a list of permitted additives. Y. Pomeranz and Clifton Meloan's *Food analysis: theory and practice* (Van Nostrand Reinhold, 1987) discusses methods, instrumentation and applications, and has an extensive bibliography.

American sources include G. A. Leveille, M. E. Zabik and K. J. Morgan, *Nutrients in foods* (Nutrition Guild, 1983) and the *Sourcebook on food and nutrition* (3rd edn, Marquis Academic Media, 1982), which gives extensive space to the problems of health that can be related to nutrition, carcinogens and food/drug interactions, and special diets.

Barbara Grigg's *The food factor* (Viking, 1986) is a lengthy but very readable account of the nutrition revolution, and considers vitamins; physical culture; and healthy eating. Food as medicine is a main theme, and topics covered include food fads; national health; whole foods; delinquency and diet; and food for the future. A good bibliography of selected major items covering the period 1850–1986 rounds off this excellent introduction to a complex subject.

The Leatherhead Food RA issues *Analytical methods manual* (2nd edn, 1987) in a loose-leaf format with regular updates; this is the best up to date summary of analytical methods conforming to International Standards Organisation and British Standards Institution practice.

ADDITIVES

As we discussed in our introduction, the question of additives in foods is one of the most urgent popular concerns; possible damage to health through consumption of "unknown" chemical additives has led to widespread consumer protest and a generally higher awareness of manufacturers' obligations to show what a food contains. There are several popular guides to this subject and Maurice Hanssen is the best known author: his *E for additives* (1984) was one of the first books in the popular market, and has now been reissued as the *New E for additives: the completely revised best selling E number guide* (Thorsons, 1987), retaining the tabular arrangement and covering colours; preservatives; anti-oxidants; emulsifiers; stabilisers; mineral hydrocarbons; and summarising its data in alphabetical lists; and with a glossary. The same author has also produced *E for additives supermarket shopping guide* (Thorsons, 1986), listing supermarket own-brand products free of prohibited additives, and indicating salt, sugar and flavouring ratings.

Other popular accounts would feature Felicity Lawrence's *Additives: your complete survival guide* (Century, 1986); and Felicity Jackson's *Taking the E out of eating* (Windward, 1986). Erik Millstone's *Food additives: taking the lid off what we really eat* (Penguin, 1986) is a useful summary of the whole topic, with interesting references; and the Ministry of Agriculture, Fisheries and Food (MAFF) has issued *Look at the label* (1984), which is a brief guide to what is permitted.

On a more substantial note, the current scene is well documented in Verner Wheelock, *Food additives in perspective* (University of Bradford, Food Policy Research Unit, 1986), which discusses the present regulations and future needs. The standard scholarly reference source is the *Handbook of food additives,* edited by Thomas E. Furia (2nd edn, CRC Press, 1972), which runs to over 1000 pages and is supplemented by a second volume issued in 1980.

3

Professional catering

The professional cook or restaurateur needs the support of a range of publications; in general there is the handling of food preparation and presentation, where to obtain supplies of commodities, how to arrange and present menus, hygiene and safety factors, and regulations applicable. Marketability of products needs also to be assessed.

GENERAL WORKS

H. L. Cracknell and R. J. Kaufmann's *Practical professional cookery* (2nd edn, Macmillan, 1981) is a good starting point; it sets out the principles of cookery on a professional basis, then considers various types of foods and how they should be handled. This is a useful source, but typographically it could be more helpfully set out. Matteo Casola's *Successful mass catering and volume feeding* (rev. edn, Continental Publications/Book Bakers, 1980) is arranged in two main sections: first managerial aspects – the organisation of the enterprise; planning; staff; merchandising; and buying; secondly the principles of mass food preparation arranged by types of food. This volume can be commended for its good layout but there are still instances of menus printed over two pages requiring a mid-menu turnover. There is a glossary of terms, charts of spices, herbs, and green condiments, and a good index.

Buffets and receptions (4th edn, Virtue, 1983) is a large glossy recipe book, well illustrated with colour plates and containing hundreds of appropriate ideas and recipes. Indexing is good, with a useful index also to national dishes. W. K. H. Bode and M. J. Leto's *Classical preparation and presentation of food* (Batsford, 1984) must be the ultimate practical guide for top-class caterers; dishes are discussed by type, menu composition is examined, culinary terms are explained, and there is a good index. The volume is illustrated with drawings and is relevant for students, apprentices and managers.

Michael Anker and Vinay Batta's *Basic restaurant theory and practice* (Longman, 1987) considers restaurant "features"; skills needed; tasks that have to be done; and carries a quantity of sound background information. The text includes revision questions, and there are useful photographs. Julia Reay's *Guide to catering organisation* (Thornes, 1983) examines the people needed; menus; planning and safety factors; and the product side — buying; storing, portion control; waste; processing; serving; also included is a section on premises and plant needed.

R. H. G. Charles, *Mass catering* (World Health Organisation Regional Office for Europe, 1983) deals with the problems, the controls and the technology — including cook/freeze; microwaving; anaerobic packing; and sections devoted to staff training; institutional catering; open-air catering; tourists and holiday camps; travel catering; and banqueting. Each section has a bibliography, and main points are summarised at the end. An admirably clear and concise publication.

Other titles that may prove valuable include D. Stevenson's *Professional cookery: the process approach* (Hutchinson, 1985) which is comprehensive and basic; Henry F. Wood, *Approach to professional cookery* (Hodder & Stoughton, 1972), is aimed at catering students, as is D. Sutherland, *Professional catering: cookery and kitchen practice* (Pitman, 1987).

Wenzel's menu maker (2nd edn, CBI Publishers, 1979) remains a classic reference volume of recipes, processes, guidelines and standards, and includes purchasing specifications and staff training information.

MENUS

Three publications that relate to menu design and presentation deserve mention: Harold Clarke, *Menu terminology* (Pergamon, 1969), is alphabetically arranged within three sections — first, culinary terms and vocabulary; secondly other aspects of terminology (processes, styles and countries), and thirdly special designations (personalities, events, hotels, clubs, restaurant specialities). A bibliography and index are included.

H. E. Visick and P. E. van Kleek's *Menu planning* (McGraw-Hill, 1974) examines menu characteristics; purchasing; balance; staffing needed; equipment; testing; costing; pricing; sales histories; and menu suggestions. Albin Seaberg, *Menu design: merchandising and marketing* (3rd edn, CBI, 1983) considers how the design of the printed menu affects customer reaction: it examines atmosphere; colour; specialities; variety; extras; how to list items; what language to use; methods of description; and concludes with many specimens; an analysis of mistakes; and advice on printing.

MANAGEMENT, PERSONNEL MANAGEMENT AND MARKETING

Several books examine the administrative side of catering; these are suitable for students preparing for examinations and for those starting up in business or anxious to improve their performance. Bernard Davis and Sally Stone's *Food and beverage management* (Heinemann, 1985) is a competent introduction covering all the basic points. J. Fuller, *Professional kitchen management* (Batsford, 1981), is an authoritative survey of good practice suitable for all sizes and types of establishment. H. V. Gullen and G. E. Rhodes's *Management in the hotel and catering industry* (Batsford, 1983) relates standard management skills to these industrial settings. P. Merrick and P. Jones's *Management of catering operations* (Cassell, 1986) is a comprehensive text with case studies and examples.

The usefulness of microcomputers as a management tool is examined by Paul Gamble, *Small computers and hospitality management* (Hutchinson Educational, 1984), which discusses available software and gives advice on how to select an appropriate machine. S. Godowski, *Microcomputers in the hotel and catering industry* (Heinemann, 1986), can also be recommended as an introduction.

Financial considerations are dealt with by Chris Ryan, *Introduction to hotel and catering economics* (Thornes, 1980), written mainly for student use; Donald Sutton, *Financial management in hotel and catering operations,* is a practical guide for all involved in this aspect.

Staff selection, training and supervision are vital in a service industry and a number of books can be used to find out about current good

34

practice. M.J. Boella, *Human resources management in the hotel and catering industry,* is a well written and comprehensive introductory text. Also of equal value are T. Hornsey and D. Dann's *Manpower management in the hotel and catering industry* (Batsford, 1984) and J. P. Magurn, *Manual of staff management in the hotel and catering industry* (Heinemann, 1977).

On a smaller scale and essentially practical are two publications of the Hotel and Catering Training Board (HCTB): *Employee relations* (1986) is a recommended text for students; and *How to recruit and select young people* (1983) analyses selection methods with useful sample forms and assessment sheets.

Marketing of catering services is the subject of another HCTB publication – *Marketing for hotels and restaurants* (1986) – offering practical advice on how to increase trade. On similar lines, J. R. Summer, *Improve your marketing techniques* (Northwood Publications) shows the relevance of general marketing strategies to the catering trade. John Shepherd's *Marketing practice in the hotel and catering industry* (Batsford, 1982) uses a series of case studies based on actual instances. R. Kotas, *Marketing orientation in the hotel and catering industry* is of general value to managers and students, and Francis Buttle, *Marketing for the hotel and catering industry,* is a thorough summary specifically aimed at the student reader.

BUYING COMMODITIES AND EQUIPMENT

The question of where to obtain supplies is of vital concern to the caterer; commodities need to be of good quality and competitively priced, and the art of knowing how to select and evaluate foods can be learnt with experience and some basic information. E. Lingard and J. Sizer's *Commodities for caterers* (Cassell, 1980) considers basic foodstuffs and discusses sources of supply; purchase methods; storage; characteristics; and variations; and relates these aspects to various foods – vegetables, fruit, dairy products, meat and fish (by type); cereals, oils, fats, herbs, colours, preservatives, beverages; and convenience foods. Diagrams are included which help in dealing with meat and fish.

Jenny Baker, *Simply fish: a guide to identifying, buying and eating fish* (Faber, 1988), features over ninety types of fish and discusses how to buy it. Advice on preparation and cooking is also given.

For catering in industrial quantities, *Food trades directory and food buyers' yearbook* (Newman Publications, annual) gives details of sources of supply for equipment and products, including non-UK producers. Brand names, wholesalers, outlets, and catering services are amongst its contents. *Frozen and chilled foods yearbook* (Retail Journals, annual) does a similar service for these more specialised areas; contractors, plant and equipment manufacturers, and suppliers are listed.

On a more domestic scale, a fascinating guide is Joy Montague, *Cook's lifeline* (Exley, 1983); this lists sources of supply for all sorts of unusual foods and products for the kitchen. Hardware, utensils, free leaflets of recipes, second-hand cookery books and gadgets are among the items included.

Purchase and preparation of local market produce is a concern of those who take overseas self-catering holidays. A series of titles from the publishers Croom Helm/Christopher Helm has explored this popular topic: titles include *Self-catering in France: making the most of local food and drink* by Arthur and Barbara Eperon (1987), which arranges its material by region; and similar titles covering *Italy* by Susan Grossman (1987); *Greece* (mainland and islands) by Florica Kyriacopoulos and Tim Salmon (1986); and *Spain and the Balearic and Canary Islands* by Carole and Chris Stewart (1986); these titles (apart from *France*) discuss local shopping; meat; fish; fruit and vegetables; extras; herbs and spices; needs of children and special diet eaters; what to take with you; and give a good selection of recipes, and glossaries of local food terms, weights and measures.

FOOD HYGIENE AND FOOD POISONING

Hygienic food handling is of the utmost importance; the results of poor hygiene are of course potentially dangerous and financially disastrous. Sources of information on the subject vary between large-scale scientific studies, and compact practical guides aimed at the prevention of problems. Richard Sprenger, *Food hygiene handbook* (3rd edn, Highfield Publications for the Institution of Environmental Health Officers, 1986), is a 40 page pamphlet that excellently summarises the topic: aspects covered include hygiene in general; poisoning; bacteria; contamination; personal hygiene; storage; preparation; premises; equipment; cleansing; and pest control. John Davenport, *Food hygiene in the catering and retail trades* (H. K. Lewis, 1982), covers similar subjects and relates its material to specific trade-catering establishments, take-away stores, vending machines, and so on. Appended are a list of organisations relevant to food hygiene; and a trade directory of materials and equipment.

Karla Longrée and Gertrude Armbruster's *Quantity food sanitation* (4th edn, Wiley, 1987) looks at problems of spoilage; micro-organisms; foodborne illnesses; storage; contamination risks; and the training of personnel. Graham Aston and John Tiffney's *Guide to improving food hygiene* (2nd edn, Northwood Books, 1981) in addition devotes space to the design of premises and equipment, and has sections for market stalls; vehicles; schools; hospitals; clubs; take-aways; meals on wheels; and on health education.

Food poisoning and food hygiene by Betty Hobbs and Richard Gilbert (5th edn, Edward Arnold, 1987) is a good introduction to the problems of food poisoning, examining cleaning of shops and other premises; infestation; bacteriology and storage care; a bibliography is included. John Trickett, *Prevention of food poisoning* (2nd edn, Thornes, 1986), is intended for students, and uses an easy-to-understand, cartoon-illustrated format. It considers various types of poisoning; where the risks lie; and how to avoid them.

Microbiology and its bearing on understanding food poisoning is examined in three authoritative sources: Thelma Parry and Rosa Pawsey's *Principles of microbiology for students of food technology* (2nd edn, Hutchinson, 1984) considers all types of micro-organisms and how to control them and discusses problems of food storage; cleaning; and concludes with a summary of relevant legislation. James Jay, *Modern food microbiology* (3rd edn, Van Nostrand Reinhold, 1986), discusses the problems of various types of foods, and surveys modern methods of food treatment, such as irradiation; a very good up to date guide. *Microbiology of frozen foods,* edited by R. K. Robinson (Elsevier Applied Science Publishers, 1985), is a series of papers discussing freezing and thawing by type of food.

The Ministry of Agriculture, Fisheries and Food (MAFF) has published *Food quality and safety: a century of progress* (HMSO, 1976), a symposium on the centenary of the Sale of Foods and Drugs Act 1875. These papers examine the development of UK legislation; the nation's diet; food analysis; US comparisons; EEC harmonisation; and consumer rights; an interesting piece of background reading.

The Leatherhead Food RA has a series of *Layman's guides,* some of which are relevant here: *Food poisoning bacteria* by A. C. Halligan and P. M. Tew (1985) describes types of poisoning and discusses how to prevent outbreaks; A. C. Halligan, *Food spoilage: the role of micro-organisms* (1986), looks at the action of bacteria, yeasts and moulds, and how to prevent spoilage. Linda Wilson, *Radioactivity: a layman's guide* (1986), is a topical contribution to another source of concern; and J. J. Rennie, *Food allergy and other food sensitivities* (1986), notes the effect that spoilage and contamination can have in cases of intolerance to various foods.

LAWS, REGULATIONS AND STANDARDS

Although complex, these topics are well documented and therefore simple to trace and examine. Some basic guides that cover all relevant UK legislation affecting the operating of the catering industries include M. Richards and S. Stewart's *Legal aspects of the hotel and catering industry* (2nd edn, Bell & Hyman, 1979); A. Pannett, *Principles of hotel and catering law* (Cassell, 1988); D. Field, *Hotel and catering law in Britain* (Sweet & Maxwell, 1982); and Frank Bull and John Hooper's *Hotel and catering law* (7th edn, Barrie & Jenkins, 1979).

The detail of food regulations and standards is admirably documented by the Leatherhead Food RA; their manual *Guide to the food regulations in the UK* (3rd edn, updated annually with supplements) is issued in a loose-leaf binder and is the authoritative source for all UK regulations. *Food additives* (3rd edn, 1982), issued in a similar manner, examines properties of all additives and lists regulations. *EEC food legislation manual* is also loose-leaf, and is updated twice a year; it covers all EEC food directives enacted or proposed, and lists permitted additives. EEC harmonisation schemes are outlined. The *Overseas food legislation manual* is updated three times a year, and covers twenty-one countries including all EEC member states; content is fully comprehensive.

The Leatherhead Food RA also offers the online database FOREGE (FOod REGulation Enquiries) which covers additives in permitted use worldwide, and has recently begun to list information on compositional standards, labelling requirements, and quality control requirements for foods in the UK, USA, Ireland, Belgium and Germany.

MARKET REPORTS

The Leatherhead Food RA is the principal source for up to the minute reports on the UK and international market for foods. *Food market updates* is a bi-monthly publication and concentrates on specific UK retail markets; recent titles have included *Fruit and vegetables in the UK* (1988); *Snack foods in the UK* (1987); *Ready meals in the UK* (1987); and *Frozen foods in the UK* (1987). Special reports concentrate on typical issues such as *Influence of increasing consumer dietary concern on the UK food and drinks market* (1986); *Impact of microwave cookers on the UK food market* (1985); *New products analysis,* which appears at regular intervals; and an annual *Year in perspective* which reviews performance of the UK food trade. *Country reports* look at data on overseas markets; recent titles have included *The US food and drinks market* (2nd edn, 1987); *Food and drink market sizes* (UK and international data sheets); and material on markets in Germany, France and Spain.

4

Training, education and careers

GENERAL

All the aspects of catering considered together cover a wide range of skills, levels of responsibility, and types of environment. Professional catering is based either in the private sphere − hotels, restaurants, pubs, clubs, holiday camps, catering departments of the travel industries; or in the "welfare" sphere, which includes school meals services, hospitals, prisons, armed forces, educational establishments and the needs of employees in shops, factories and offices.

Basic education and training for catering work involves management of people; planning and organisation of equipment and premises; selection and purchase of commodities and other raw materials; preparation; quality control; and service of food; the training and supervision of other staff and immediate handling of problems as they arise. These aspects will feature to some extent in the work of every caterer, whether the manager of a hotel or large catering operation who will concentrate on quality through management and training of others, or the small caterer running a bistro or sandwich bar whose responsibilities will be more inclined to personal involvement in purchase and preparation. The amateur cook will also need to think about purchase of commodities, preparation and serving, and may be concerned to attend a course to learn more, or develop skills in areas of interest.

Qualification levels in hotel and catering management ("Hospitality

Management") range from degree courses at a small number of universities, several polytechnics and other colleges of higher education, often including a period of field work or industrial release; to a variety of simpler courses. Polytechnics and further education colleges operate a variety of BTEC National and Higher National courses, offering craft and supervisory skills in this subject area. City and Guilds of London Institute examinations also cover the craft level, and are widely available in Further Education colleges; the BTEC First Certificate is also now offered, leading on to the National diploma course if required. The Hotel and Catering Industry Management Association (HCIMA) is the professional body for managers in all sections of the industry, and a professional qualification is offered.

Special qualifications are available for dietitians, nutritional specialists and various relevant medical sub-professions; it is beyond the scope of this book to deal in these specialities and reference should be made to local careers libraries or the careers services of schools and colleges. A number of courses in the field of Home Economics also include an element of catering teaching, and some readers who wish to think about cookery as a part of a wider range of activities could investigate this with careers officers. Julie Fish's book *Careers in home economics* (2nd edn, Kogan Page, 1987) explains the range of options open in the food industry; retailing; teaching; research; consumer education; and communications. Courses at all levels are listed with details of relevant establishments extending to over 30 pages, and there is a section containing the addresses of appropriate professional bodies and other organisations.

CAREERS IN CATERING

The principal decision to be made when considering catering as a career is whether to work for an employer, or whether to work on a self-employed basis. Standard careers sources discuss mainly the former alternative, whereas published literature tends to be devoted more to self-employment.

A basic guide is John Kinross, *Careers in catering and hotel management* (2nd edn, Kogan Page, 1985) which includes information on a variety of career possibilities; full details of opportunities for training and qualification; an assessment of career prospects; working conditions; and advice on how to apply for jobs. Details of relevant organisations and a list of recognised courses are also appended.

The government-funded Careers and Occupational Information Centre (COIC) publish an annual guide entitled *Occupations;* this is a valuable compendium of advice on all types of career opportunities and includes a section "Catering and other services" (Group I in the classification system in the volume). *Occupations* recognises three sectors of relevant employment: commercial, welfare, and armed forces; and an introductory section discusses possibilities and gives substantial background information. Various categories are then examined: hotel manager; catering manager; housekeeper; chef/cook; kitchen assistant; waiter/waitress; and counter service assistant. For each occupation a description is provided covering the nature of the work, environment, pay and conditions, opportunities, prospects, personal characteristics needed, entry requirements and full details of training and qualifications at all levels. Information on late entry into catering careers, related jobs, and names of organisations is also given.

Among other series published by COIC, basic information for craft levels of employment is included in the *If I were* series; these single-sheet guides are very simple and give only the most fundamental data. Titles relevant to this subject include *Baker/confectioner* (no. 91); *Waiter/waitress* (no. 40); *Cook/chef* (no. 26); and *Butcher* (no. 22). COIC's *Job outlines* series gives fuller details of the range of careers and the skills and qualifications needed; these titles are packed with valuable data and represent a good comprehensive introduction. *Hotel and catering* (1983) is no. 23 in the series, and *Home economics* (1986) is no. 105.

More information at a basic level is available in Fleur Hogarth, *Jobs in hotels* (2nd edn, Kogan Page, 1988), which covers jobs such as chef, waiter and kitchen assistant; or Joy Lennick, *Jobs in baking and confectionery* (2nd edn, Kogan Page, 1987).

The Hotel and Catering Industry Management Association (HCIMA) is the professional body for managers, trainee managers and students aiming at careers in these fields; all types of employing organisations and self-employment are included. HCIMA provides to its members information on educational qualifications and courses, careers, salaries and conditions of employment. Membership would also be needed to take advantage of HCIMA information and appointment services.

The Hotel and Catering Training Board (HCTB) Research Unit publishes several items important in career selection; these include

Women in the hotel and catering industry (1987); and *Hotel and catering manpower in Britain 1984* (1985). These and other research publications present data on the size of the workforce, skills needed, and developments likely to affect employment prospects.

SELF-EMPLOYMENT

Most of the sources we have mentioned in the preceding section deal in part with opportunities for self-employment in the catering industry, but there are additionally several titles aimed at the would-be restaurateur or caterer. A selection of titles would include Colin Cooper English, *Thinking of buying a restaurant?* (David and Charles, 1983), which deals with finance and property matters; equipment; staff; publicity; and the role of microcomputers; and *Running your own restaurant* by Diane Hughes and Godfrey Golzen (Kogan Page, 1986) which is similarly comprehensive.

Other standard sources for this type of work are Peter Douglas, *Run your own restaurant* (Harrap, 1976); and David Miller, *Starting a small restaurant* (rev. edn, Harvard Common Press, 1983). Ursula Garner and Judy Ridgway's *Running your own catering business* (Kogan Page, 1984) examines other means of catering outside the restaurant environment; and useful material will also be found in Joy Lennick, *Running your own small hotel* (2nd edn, Kogan Page, 1988).

For those who wish to offer catering services on a less formal basis, Michelle Berriedale-Johnson, *Cook for hire* (Macdonald Orbis, 1987), offers basic advice on setting up, with examples of functions and menus; and Jennifer Curry, *Cooking for Cash* (David & Charles, 1983), discusses cafés, parties and buffets, banquets and dinner parties – providing catering services on other people's premises for functions and events.

TRAINING MATERIALS

The Hotel and Catering Training Board (HCTB) publishes many videos, packages and booklets designed for the training of catering staff, managers and supervisors in all branches of the industry. These may be used to support organised courses, or for in-service training schemes, or for use in specific training applications in an individual workplace.

Materials are produced to a high standard — videos feature professional actors, sometimes very well-known names, and are accompanied by trainers' notes and support literature.

The selection of videos available includes such titles as *Cooking on another wavelength* (1984), which discusses the possibilities of microwave cookery; *Culinary practice* (1984), which examines good food preparation methods; *Gerry the germ* (1982), concerned with food hygiene; *Great expectations* (1985), which looks at restaurant service from the customer's viewpoint; and *Pilgrim's progress* (1985), which considers the problem facing a restaurant manager who has no supervisory or managerial experience and demonstrates how staff goodwill and loyalty can be developed.

HCTB training literature comprises many attractively produced, well illustrated booklets; *About kitchen safety* (published with Scriptographic Publications, 1984) is in a cartoon style format; *Fish for caterers* (published with the Sea Fish Industry Authority, 1984) covers selection, preparation, cooking and presentation and includes several recipes; other titles relate to hygiene and safety factors, starting up a business, and various guidelines on teaching and training aids.

A new HCTB venture in partnership with Macmillan Education Ltd is a series of Mastercraft Study Books and Videos, which concentrate on various aspects of catering operations, food preparation and service. Titles include the *Professional kitchen;* the *Meat programme; Pastries and cakes* (all published 1987) in the Foodcraft Video section; and Mastercraft Study Books include volumes on *Dry processes* including baking, roasting, grilling and so on; and *Wet processes,* including boiling, stewing, cook/chill and cook/freeze (both 1988). These follow the syllabuses of various City and Guilds examinations.

John Fuller and A. J. Currie's *The waiter* (3rd edn, Hutchinson, 1965 and subsequent reprints) is a standard training text, covering all aspects of food service — equipment; menus; service preparation; reception of guests; all types of functions; and relates to most situations from restaurant practice to snack bars.

QUALIFICATIONS AND EDUCATIONAL COURSES

As we explained in the Careers section above, the range of levels of work in the catering industry extends from manual trades to high-level management. Consequently the range of educational courses and qualifications available cover a wide spectrum of abilities. The standard guide to courses in all subjects, is *DOFE (Directory of further and many higher education courses in the UK)* (CRAC/Hobsons Publishing, annual) which covers polytechnics and colleges, and lists courses that are full-time, part-time, block release, day release; and range in level from degree and professional qualification courses to BTEC, City and Guilds, A-level and GCSE courses. Introductory sections of the volume give details of background and accrediting bodies; then course listings show a regional key so that courses in a given area can be selected. The section "Catering, hotel-keeping, food service, and homecrafts" covers general catering; professional cookery; home crafts and management; and food science/technology, which includes dietetics and nutrition. The list of courses is arranged first by level of qualification, then format (full-time, day release, and so on), then by name of college.

The *Directory of catering education and training* (HCTB, 1985) covers our field specifically and includes information on courses; qualifications; training initiatives; government schemes; award-making bodies; and professional associations. Diagrams of the structure of routes and qualifications are provided and throughout there are contact addresses and telephone numbers. HCTB also produces a *College list* (5th edn, 1987) which gives details of courses in UK universities, polytechnics and colleges. Roy Hayter, *A career in catering: choosing a course* (Pergamon, 1980), is also a valuable source.

HCTB now offers an open learning management programme, in which nine self-study units are taken at the candidate's own pace and give a thorough grounding in management without formal tuition, time off work, or entry qualifications; marketing, financial control, management software and personnel management are included. HCTB also offers craft level awards, one of which − Caterbase − is a Modular scheme using the Mastercraft Study Books and Videos mentioned above; operational management and business management training programmes are also offered. HCIMA offers a professional qualification based on its own examinations or the equivalent diploma or degree level awards of related organisations.

Short courses are offered by a number of organisations; the Leatherhead Food RA offers a comprehensive annual programme of one-, two- or three-day courses on topics such as health and nutrition; developing a cleaning programme; manufacture of pickles and sauces; quality of meat pies; fish farming; and manufacture of chocolate confectionery, all of which feature in the 1988 programme of some sixty events. HCTB and colleges also offer short courses on subjects of topical interest.

Private centres, colleges and schools also flourish, and advertise themselves in magazines and Sunday newspapers; Cordon Bleu cookery and other fashionable styles are the usual topics, and courses may be of single-day duration, or longer periods leading to the school's own diploma or certificate. Standards vary, so care should be taken over the selection of such establishments; the better ones are outstanding for the quality of their work.

5

Home cooking

LEARNING TO COOK

Almost everyone needs to learn to cook at some time in their lives, and though it is possible to learn by trial and error, it is easier if some of the basic skills are learned more systematically at the outset, as many recipe books assume their users know how to make a white sauce or shortcrust pastry. There are a number of reliable books available which provide step-by-step instructions and background information.

A useful and well-established text is *Practical cookery* by Victor Ceserani and Ronald Kinton, first published in 1962 and now in its sixth edition (Edward Arnold, 1987). It is written for catering students and gives information on different types of food and cooking processes. The large collection of classic amd modern recipes is suitable for domestic use as each recipe is worked on a four-portion basis. It is a good introduction to the principles of cookery for any amateur who wants more than step-by-step recipe books. A thorough and popular work is *Delia Smith's cookery course,* based on the BBC television series, available in three parts (BBC, 1978, 1979, 1981), or in one volume (BBC, 1982) which does not easily stay open at the required page. It is geared to the complete beginner but with recipes and techniques that the experienced cook can gain from, and works step-by-step through different foodstuffs and cookery methods, with over 500 recipes. Elisabeth Ayrton, *Good simple cookery* (Macdonald, 1984), has been a popular work since 1958 and covers traditional cooking in a straightforward way. It is aimed at the beginner, but has an interesting range of recipes that should also suit more experienced cooks. Another reliable work from the Good Housekeeping canon is *The Good Housekeeping step-by-step cook book,* edited by G. Edden (Ebury Press, 1980). It describes techniques, equipment, preparation methods and entertaining, and has a good recipe collection arranged under headings such as: vegetables; fruit; desserts; cakes; and pasta; with an excellent introduction to each section.

Some of the published "cookery courses" concentrate on gourmet dishes, though using the same step-by-step methods as the more basic cookery books. Prue Leith (a well-known restaurateur and cookery writer) and Caroline Waldegrave, *Leith's cookery school* (Macdonald, 1985), is a collection of graded "menu lessons" each with recipes and a full description of methods and techniques. The food is relatively rich and expensive, though the authors have taken care to balance menus nutritionally and to consider colour and texture in presentation. The techniques are demanding and the book needs to be used by an experienced and enthusiastic cook. *Master class for creative cooks* by Evelyn Rose and Sula Leon (Piatkus, 1987) is a collection of recipes arising from the authors' cookery classes and demonstrations, and includes classic, unusual and exotic dishes.

There are so many step-by-step and pictorial guides to cooking that it is impossible to cover them all here, but many of the recipe compendia examined in the following section also contain basic information on method and techniques.

RECIPE COMPENDIA

There are hundreds of general recipe books available, and though all works are selective, a compendium of recipes can be expected to cover all types of food and more or less the full range of cooking methods. It is useful to own one, even if individual tastes then require that more specific cookbooks are purchased or borrowed. *Purnell's complete cookery* edited by A. London (Purnell, 1974) is enormous, containing over 8000 recipes with thousands of illustrations demonstrating step-by-step techniques or the finished dish. There is a lot of information on techniques and presentation; and an excellent subject index. Some sections on their own would be material for a small book; there are 14 large format pages on sandwiches, for example. There are gaps in coverage – vegetarian cuisine is unacknowledged in the index, for instance, although there are plenty of vegetable recipes that could be used as main dishes. The Good Housekeeping Institute's *Good Housekeeping cookery book* (12th rev. edn, Ebury, 1985) started life in 1948 and is fully revised and updated; coverage is wide-ranging and thorough with plenty of information on cooking techniques. The layout is clear and well organised. Two basic and inexpensive publications are the *All colour cookbook* (Hamlyn, 1970); and the *New all colour cookbook* (Hamlyn, 1986). Both cover the full range of recipes – soups, snacks and starters; fish; meat; vegetarian meals; desserts and baking; and the layout is clear and easy to use with a colour photograph of each dish and the recipe beneath. A more substantial work of over 500 pages is *Good cooking made easy* (Hamlyn, 1986) with a range of recipes from everyday eating to dinner parties. Symbols indicate preparation time, cost, and level of difficulty. A collection of over 450 recipes towards the gourmet end of the spectrum is to be found in *Great cooking: the best recipes from Time-Life books* (Time-Life, 1987).

HISTORICAL RECIPES

Written recipes and recipe books have been traced to almost all periods and places where men and women with writing skills have lived. Over the centuries, within regions and countries, characteristic cuisines have developed, and with them a literature not only of recipes but of the philosophy of food. In this century considerable interest has been shown in original recipes from other times and cultures; compilations of such recipes exist, often adapted for use by the modern cook.

One of the most recent historical recipe collections is, appropriately, *The British Museum cookbook* compiled by Michelle Berriedale-Johnson (British Museum, 1987). It recreates over 100 recipes from early cultures such as Ancient Egypt, Medieval Europe and Imperial China. Each section gives an overview of the style of cooking and an authentic menu. The recipes are usable, though the quantities may be daunting (4½lb mussels for a Caudel of musculs, or a bulky 3lb fresh spinach). *Elinor Fettiplace's receipt book: Elizabethan country house cooking,* edited by Hilary Spurling (Viking Salamander, 1986) is an early and therefore more exotic form of what we now regard as traditional English cooking. The recipes come from an early seventeenth-century Oxfordshire household, and were collected by Lady Elinor from friends, neighbours and relations. Arranged by month, the recipes and descriptions are interpreted for modern usage by the editor, who has chosen to retain the Elizabethan spelling. The recipes in their original form are vague as to measures and quantities as early and personal records tend to be, so as a working cookbook it is not easy to use, but it is full of historical interest. Samuel Pepys enjoyed food among his other pleasures, and compiled from comments and descriptions in his diaries comes *Pepys at table: seventeenth-century recipes for the modern cook* compiled by Christopher Driver and Michelle Berriedale-Johnson (Bell & Hyman, 1984). As the title indicates, recipes are adapted or structured from loose descriptions for modern use. *Margaretta Acworth's Georgian cookery book* (Pavilion Books, 1987) is an updated transcription of over 100 recipes selected from 400 discovered in the Public Record Office. The editors, Alice and Frank Prochaska, have also provided advice on contemporary (eighteenth-century) food presentation. Recipes from *Mrs Beeton's book of household management* (various editions, described below in the section on British cooking) provides a first-hand account of Victorian family eating habits and tastes. Mrs Beeton does indulge in the middle-class dietary excesses of the period however, and another contemporary work gives an insight into how the "lower orders" might have eaten: *A plain cookery book for the working classes* by Charles Francatelli (Chief Cook to Her Majesty the Queen) was published by Routledge, Warne and Routledge towards the middle of the nineteenth century, with the aim "to show you how you may prepare and cook your daily food, so as to obtain from it the greatest amount of nourishment at the least possible expense". The 1852 edition was reprinted in facsimile by Scolar Press in 1977. In our own century, rationing, the complete absence of some foodstuffs and the introduction of new ones, gave cooking during the Second World War a characteristic flavour. This is captured in two books, both illustrated with memorabilia from the war years. *We'll eat again* compiled by Marguerite Patten in association with the Imperial War Museum (Hamlyn, 1985), and Bryan Chalker, *Cook-ups of World War Two* (Redcliffe Press, 1987), offer the nutritious and economical if sometimes surprising recipes that developed from the imposed limitations and guidelines emanating from the Ministry of Food, Potato Pete and Dr Carrot. A classic *general* history of English food, packed with descriptions of English life, kitchen and cooking equipment and utensils, anecdotes, quotations, and hundreds of original recipes, is

Dorothy Hartley, *Food in England,* first published in 1954 and now available as a paperback (Futura, 1985).

INGREDIENTS

There are hundreds of recipe books available which concentrate on one specific ingredient (such as chocolate) or a category of ingredients (such as vegetables). This section examines some examples of published works to demonstrate their scope and range.

Vegetables

An excellent reference work is *Jane Grigson's vegetable book* (Michael Joseph, 1978); any book with a 36 page index which cross-references over 550 pages of text has to be considered a standard work. It is organised alphabetically by vegetable and provides information on the history and preparation of each as well as recipes. Nika Hazelton, *Vegetable cookery,* in the Penguin Handbooks series (Penguin, 1979) is also arranged by vegetable with advice on how to buy and store, and on nutritional values. Recipes from all parts of the world but where "a specific vegetable is the main ingredient" are provided. An inexpensive and basic guide is *Vegetable cookery* (Hamlyn, 1986) with advice on how to use each vegetable, and sections on starters; canapés; soups; main dishes; salads; marinades; dressings and vinegars; cakes and desserts; and drinks. Offering more sophisticated ideas is Patricia Bourne, *French vegetable cookery: traditional and regional recipes* (Macdonald, 1985). It offers recipes for vegetables on their own; as accompaniments to meat and fish; as vegetarian dishes; and in sweets. There are very full sections on hors-d'oeuvres, soufflés, pancakes and quiches. There is more emphasis on seasoning and sauces than is traditional in British cooking. John Tovey (of the Miller Howe Restaurant) concentrates on vegetables as accompaniments in his *Feast of vegetables: the perfect accompaniment to any meal* (Century, 1985). As well as all the familiar standards such as cabbage and carrots, he encourages us to use dandelion, hop shoots and pumpkin as well as increasingly familiar exotics such as aubergines and okra. Dried pulses are the focus of *The bean book* by Rose Elliot (Fontana, 1979); and *Bean feast* by Pamela Westland (Granada, 1981). The former is vegetarian in principle; the latter uses meat where appropriate.

Exotic vegetables are covered in many of the books mentioned above, but are specifically though briefly described, with recipes, in Rosamond Richardson, *The little exotic vegetable book* (Piatkus, 1987). This series covers other vegetables such as avocados, garlic, and mushrooms and potatoes. More exotic than "the exotics" are the vegetable subjects of Peter Bradford's *Cooking with sea vegetables* (Thorsons, 1985), a clear and explanatory work which covers the use of the familiar dulse and carrageen as well as less known foods such as the Japanese seaweeds.

The great garlic cookbook by Sophie Hale (Apple Press, 1986) confines itself to recipes using that flavouring vegetable, and does so in sweets (garlic fudge) and refreshers (lime and garlic granita) as well as in more conventional dishes. N. and M. Addinall, *Wild mushrooms; how to find, identify and cook them* (Davies, 1987), aims to help the user distinguish mushrooms of gastronomic value from their inedible or poisonous colleagues, and gives advice on cooking and serving.

Fruit

Jane Grigson and Charlotte Knox, *Exotic fruits and vegetables* (Cape, 1986), offers background information and advice on recognition and preparation of the exotic fruits, vegetables and spices readily available in supermarkets, along with a range of recipes. A very thorough work on all types of fruit is Pam Cary, *The fresh fruit cookbook* (Crowood Press, 1988), with recipes for starters and main courses as well as puddings, using traditional apples and pears, soft and citrus fruits, and the exotic and imported. Susan Fleming, *The little exotic fruit book* (Piatkus, 1987), provides facts and recipes on twenty-five of the readily available exotic fruits. *The compleat strawberry* by Stafford Whiteaker (Century, 1985) is one of the few books available that deals exclusively with one fruit, and covers the history, cosmetic uses, and use in art and advertising as well as food use. Books in the "Little books" series (Piatkus) give facts and recipes on the strawberry, the lemon, and the apple.

Grains

Arto der Haroutunian, *The whole grain cookbook* (Pan, 1987), is perhaps the most thorough work available on grain cookery, and offers a wide range of recipes from the most appropriate of the world's cuisines for rice, wheat, barley, buckwheat, millet and rye. Oats are part of the British tradition and have a high nutritional content; recipes for all kinds of dishes including soups, main courses and desserts are offered in Pamela Westland's *Oat cuisine* (Ward Lock, 1985), and Mary Cadogan and Shirley Bond, *The oat cookbook* (Optima, 1987).

Fish and seafood

Some of the most thorough fish cookery books available are those by Alan Davidson, discussed below in the regional cookery section; they consist of an alphabetical descriptive catalogue of fish and supporting recipes for each region. A general and inexpensive introduction to this topic is *The WI book of fish and seafood* by Mary Norwak (Ebury, 1987), a collection of over 100 tried and tested recipes. Based on the BBC television series, Keith Floyd's *Floyd on fish* (BBC, 1985) is informative and original in its approach to handling and cooking fish, and is an excellent introduction to basic and more imaginative fish cookery. The section on choosing and preparing fish is succinct and illustrated with clear diagrams; there are recipes for butters, stocks and sauces to use with fish; and the fish recipes, though anecdotal, are clearly explained.

Meat, poultry and game

Another inexpensive Women's Institute guide is *The WI book of meat cookery* by Angela Mottram (Ebury, 1986), a collection of recipes using the full range of methods of cooking meat, backed up by practical information. There are many very specialised books on meat cookery. *Fresh ways with beef and veal* (Time-Life, 1988) aims, through its recipes, to reduce fat and cholesterol intake for meat eaters. Unusual vegetable accompaniments are suggested. Antony and Araminta Hippisley Coxe's *Book of sausages* (Gollancz, 1987) suggests ways to use sausages from all over the world, and has a section devoted to sausage-making. It contains an amazing range of recipes. *Offal* (Time-Life, 1981) is organised by cooking method, and provides recipes for poaching, braising, sautéeing, and grilling offal; there is also a section on sausage-making. It is clearly set out with step-by-step photographic illustrations accompanying the more difficult recipes.

Judy Ridgway, *101 quick ways with chicken* (Piatkus, 1987), is a collection of recipes organised by cooking time (from fifteen minutes to one hour).

Two game cookery books are discussed in the Scottish regional cookery section. In addition to those, Colin Brown, *The game cookbook* (Souvenir, 1986), covers wild boar and goat as well as the more usual indigenous game, and offers recipes for soups and entrées as well as banquet and gourmet dishes. Angela Humphreys, *Game cookery* (David & Charles, 1986), is a practical work that tells the user how to deal with either oven-ready or furred or feathered game, and using either microwave or a conventional oven. The range of recipes will suit a complete beginner as well as the more experienced cook.

Dairy products

The real cheese cookbook by Catherine Clavell (Windward, 1987) is an international alphabetical catalogue of cheeses, with a collection of recipes covering the full range of dishes including desserts. Judy Ridgway, *The complete cheese cookbook* (Piatkus, 1986), is also a guide to the world's cheeses and offers over 200 recipes for classic dishes. Lucy Handly, *The book of cheesecakes* (Salamander, 1988), uses a wide variety of cheeses in 100 recipes for both sweet and savoury cheesecakes.

Basic egg recipes along with facts, tips and quotations are provided by Jenny Ridgway in *The little egg book* (Piatkus, 1987). Omelettes, blinis, crêpes and pancakes are the subject of Mary Norwak's *The book of crêpes and omelettes* (Salamander, 1987), with a range of recipes for fillings.

Cheese, eggs, butter, milk and yoghurt are the focus of *The dairy book of family cookery,* published on behalf of the Milk Marketing Board (Ebury Press, 1983), which contains over 700 recipes for soups, starters, and appetisers; main courses; sauces; snacks; desserts (including 17 recipes for ice creams) and baking; and "young eats". It is an attractive book with clear recipes, but not one to be used too frequently by the calorie-conscious!

Pasta

Though the Italian cookery books discussed in the regional section cover pasta and pasta dishes very thoroughly, individual books on pasta have their uses. A heavily illustrated and relatively expensive work is Antonio Piccinardi's *Taste of pasta* (Webb & Bower, 1987) which contains 122 recipes for cheese, meat, fish and vegetable pasta dishes. The traditional recipes are represented, and there are many more elaborate recipes using the techniques of nouvelle cuisine. *Fresh ways with pasta* (Time-Life, 1987) has instructions for making pasta at home and advice on microwave cooking as well as a range of attractive recipes. A good introductory work is *The book of pasta* by Lesley Mackley (Salamander, 1987) which contains not only the traditional Italian dishes, but also pasta-using recipes from elsewhere in the world. Desserts as well as savoury dishes are featured.

What might almost be called a "fast pasta" book is *The top 100 pasta sauces* by Diane Seed (Rosendale Press, 1987). It provides recipes for vegetable, fish and shellfish, cheese, and meat sauces, most of which can be prepared very simply and quickly. The section of "special occasion" recipes is rather more demanding, but all recipes are clearly presented and explained, and the overall impression from the book is of a fresh and healthy range of dishes (Figure 5.1).

Chocolate

There seems to have been a spate of chocolate books in the last few years. One of the first was *The chocolate book* by Helge Rubinstein (Macdonald, 1981), written "for chocoholics everywhere . . .". It is a collection of sweet and savoury dishes from the simple to the complex, intermingled with the history of chocolate, quotations about it, and illustrations based on old advertisements, labels and engravings. Jennie Reekie, *The ultimate chocolate cookbook* (Ward Lock, 1983), offers practical recipes for sweets, cakes and biscuits, hot and cold puddings, ices, sauces and drinks. *The great chocolate book* (Absolute Press, 1986) is a collection of cake and dessert recipes − most of which require time and patience − from British and Irish cooks. Chocolate as an icing and decoration is covered in Pat Ashby's *Chocolate* (Merehurst Press, 1986), which includes making Easter eggs and decorations. The different types of chocolate and their uses are described, and techniques of melting and cooling are clearly outlined. Making Easter eggs is also discussed in *The book of chocolates and petit fours* by Beverley Sutherland Smith (Salamander, 1986) along with making filled and moulded chocolates and chocolate-coated nuts. Both of these books are aimed at the home cook using basic equipment.

For those who must not or should not eat chocolate there is *The Here's Health alternative chocolate book: over 100 healthy carob recipes* by Janette Marshall (Century, 1986). Ten chocolate classics

Figure 5.1   Fast pasta recipes clearly presented and explained

Source: Diane Seed, *The top 100 pasta sauces,* illus. Robert Budwig (Rosendale Press, 1987), p. 27. Reproduced by kind permission of Rosendale Press.

(such as chocolate mousse, Black Forest gâteau and profiteroles) are recreated, and there are recipes for cakes, biscuits, puddings and drinks.

Herbs and spices

Herbs and spices are an ancient element in cooking because of their preservative, medicinal and flavouring properties. Herbals — books listing and describing herbs and their properties — are also long established. One of the most famous English herbals is John Gerard's *Herball, or general historie of plants,* first published in 1597 but best known in the edition of 1636. It is available as a facsimile (*Gerard's Herball,* new edn, Dover, 1975); or in an edited and shortened version (Bracken Books, 1985). Though its primary aim is to identify and decribe medical properties, food uses and cooking methods are sometimes described and give an interesting insight into sixteenth-century eating habits and tastes.

Most of the modern cookery books specialising in herbs and spices provide a section listing and describing the plants and their properties, and most are attractively (though not necessarily usefully) illustrated. Some books deal only with spices (the fruits or seeds of plants, used whole or ground). The classic work is probably Elizabeth David's *Spices, salts and aromatics in the English kitchen* (new edn, Penguin, 1987), first published in 1970. The author explains the historic influence of the oriental spice trade on English cooking, and provides recipes from all over the world and all periods of history, adapted to modern British cooking methods. It is an excellent collection covering sauces, fish, meat and poultry dishes; puddings and cakes; chutneys, pickles and beverages. The thorough bibliography and reading list make it a scholarly as well as a practical tool. *Cooking with spices* by Carolyn Heal and Michael Allsop (David & Charles, 1983) is arranged alphabetically by type of spice rather than type of recipe, which is useful if the user has bought a new spice and wishes to try it. Equally useful is the very thorough index allowing access to recipes by chief ingredient. Each spice is fully described, and there are notes on preparation and storage, uses, chemical composition, properties, and cultivation, as well as recipes, a foreign language glossary, a spice map, and notes on spice mixtures. Among the books specifically on herbs, an inexpensive and nicely produced one is *The herb book* by Arabella Boxer and Philippa Slack (new edn, Peerage, 1985; Hamlyn, 1987). It is a guide to the history, cultivation and uses of herbs, and contains nearly 300 recipes created by Arabella Boxer for soups; fish, meat, poultry and game main courses; vegetable and vegetarian dishes; salads; breads and cakes; and drinks. A nice period piece is Mrs C. F. Leyel's *Herbal delights; tisanes, syrups, confections, electuaries, rubs, juleps, vinegars and conserves* (new edn, Faber, 1987) originally published in 1937.

A good basic work on both herbs and spices is the Good Housekeeping Institute's *Cooking with herbs and spices* (Ebury Press, 1975), out of print at the time of writing, but worth looking out for. It covers how to grow and store herbs, and there are over 200 clearly presented recipes for starters; main meals; salads; desserts; cakes and biscuits. Sarah Garland, *The herb and spice book* (Frances Lincoln/Weidenfeld & Nicolson, 1979), is again more than a recipe book − in fact the recipe section is no more than one-fifth of the book − but is imaginative, and usefully organised under quite narrow headings such as soups; eggs; butters and cheeses; and pasta. Gail Duff's *Book of herbs and spices: recipes, remedies and lore* (Merehurst Press, 1987) concentrates on thirty herbs and twenty spices and provides a collection of classic recipes that combine food and seasoning in a traditional manner. An inexpensive and basic but very practical little book is *Cooking with herbs and spices* (Colour Library, 1987), a collection of recipes for soups; meat, poultry and game; fish and seafood; rice and pasta; cheese; eggs; vegetables and salads; cakes; biscuits; desserts and preserves.

Flowers

Flowers can be eaten either for their flavour or as edible decorations. Two recent books are useful in providing suggestions for their use. Jenny Leggatt, *Cooking with flowers: bring your garden into the kitchen with over 150 delicious recipes* (Century, 1987), lists edible flowers and gives information on their growing, gathering, drying and storing. The recipes are predominantly for savoury dishes. There is also information on complementary table decoration, and party menus. A very pretty book is Claire Clifton's *Edible flowers* (Bodley Head, 1983), well illustrated with colour paintings by Glynn Boyd Harte. It is an interesting collection of 20 savoury, 17 sweet, and 20 "spirituous" recipes. Both books describe the technique of crystallising flowers.

Food from the wild

The classic work on this topic is Richard Mabey's *Food for free* (new edn, paperback, Fontana, 1975; new edn, boards, Peerage, 1986), first published in 1972, which helps the reader locate, identify and use nuts, berries, leafy plants, fungi and other products of field and hedgerow. A more conventional recipe book however is *The wildfoods cookbook* by Joy O. I. Spoczynska (Hale, 1985). It is organised by foodstuff, with chapters on nettles, dandelions, roots, fruits and berries, nuts, and so on; there are 12 recipes for chickweed alone. Other useful books are Rosamond Richardson, *Hedgerow cookery* (Penguin, 1980), and J. Urquhart, *Food from the wild* (David & Charles, 1978). A marine equivalent to the above books is *Food from the seashore* by Kendall McDonald (Pelham, 1980). It is a thorough guide to locating, catching, identifying and preparing for the table foods such as lobsters, crabs, prawns, shrimps, mussels and cockles, clams, limpets, whelks, winkles and seaweed. There are not a lot of recipes for the foods once prepared, but these can be found elsewhere.

RECIPES FOR SPECIAL COOKING METHODS

Baking

Baking — the technique of cooking with dry heat, usually in an enclosed oven — is used for dough, pastry, cake and biscuit recipes. One of the classic bread books, outlining its history and principles as well as providing recipes, is *English bread and yeast cookery* by Elizabeth David (Allen Lane, 1977). Almost 600 pages, and with a huge collection of recipes for traditional breads and yeast baking, it is an essential and standard work. An inexpensive but useful basic guide to the art of making scones, breads and other yeast doughs is *Baking and bread* by Mitzie Wilson and Nichola Palmer (Hamlyn, 1987), which provides a lot of information in the brief scope of 64 pages. Beverley Sutherland Smith, *Bread and beyond: original bread recipes for every occasion* (Orbis, 1986), explains the principles and techniques involved in making and shaping breads. There are recipes using white, wholemeal and rye flours, in plain and rich doughs. A more specialised bread book is Virginia T. Habeeb's *Pita the great* (Ebury, 1986), a collection of recipes for the now familiar and popular Middle Eastern pita breads, and a range of fillings. A further extension of bread dough is the pizza, and a nice collection of recipes for pizza dough and toppings can be found in Vincenzo Buonassisi's *Pizza plus* (Collins, 1984); it also covers other national specialities with similar dough bases.

All the above books concentrate on baking breads and other yeast dough mixes. The scope is widened in *The country bakehouse: traditional baking from the country kitchen* by Christopher Conil (Crowood Press, 1988). It provides a collection of regional recipes which include breads, cakes, savouries, snacks, biscuits, and baked puddings and desserts. *Baking: step-by-step to perfect cakes, pastries and bread* (Hamlyn, 1986) is a substantial guide to baking, illustrated with 1000 colour photographs. Each section describes and illustrates a basic process using a relatively simple recipe, and then provides illustrated recipes for more complex items using the newly learned skills. Biscuits are thoroughly covered in *The WI book of biscuits: over 100 recipes tried and tested by the Women's Institute* (Ebury Press, 1984), though the recipes are mainly for traditional "white flour" biscuits. *Delia Smith's book of cakes* (rev. edn, Hodder & Stoughton, 1987) offers over 100 recipes for traditional and new cakes, from plain to elaborate, and is written in her customary straightforward and practical style with plenty of information on equipment and methods. Much more specialised are works such as Pam Dotter, *Miniature cakes, pastries and desserts* (Pelham, 1987); and Elaine MacGregor, *Wedding cakes* (Merehurst Press, 1988), with recipes and instructions for twenty-five wedding cakes based on ten different shapes of tin.

Pies are a very popular baked food, and the *National Trust book of pies* (David & Charles, 1987) is discussed below in the section on English cooking. There are two older and wider-ranging works well worth looking at by the pie enthusiast. Mary Norwak, *The pie book* (Michael Joseph, 1975), offers recipes for a range of pastries and fillings for double crust, single crust, deep and plate pies, of sweet and savoury kinds. *The pie book* by Louis de Gouy (Dover, 1949 (1974)) contains 419 characteristically American recipes for sweet pies such as cherry mince meat pie, English toffee pie, pecan pie and pineapple marshmallow pie.

Microwave cooking

The Good Housekeeping Institute has produced a number of books about microwave cooking, some general, others more specialised, but all very clear and informative. The most basic introductory work for the novice microwave cook is the *Good Housekeeping microwave handbook* (2nd edn, Ebury Press, 1986). This contains information on techniques and menu-planning, and provides cooking charts, easy sample recipes, and a range of more standard recipes. *The Good Housekeeping microwave encyclopaedia* by Susanna Tee (Ebury Press, 1986) has 350 recipes for the full range of dishes including snacks, soups and preserves, dishes for one or two people; and a lot of background information on method and equipment. *Good Housekeeping family microwave cookery* (Ebury Press, 1985) has over 150 recipes including baked items, but is particularly excellent in its introductory section which explains the principles of microwave cookers and cookery. Another helpful basic general work is *Mary Berry's favourite microwave recipes* (Piatkus, 1987) which tells you what the cooker can and cannot do, and provides almost 100 recipes.

There are a number of more specialised works available of which the following are examples. Marguerite Patten, *Microwave for one* (Hamlyn, 1987), is an inexpensive guide to the use of the microwave for drinks, snacks and full meals in the one-person household. Healthy eating is the focus of Janet Smith's *Good Housekeeping microwave fish cookbook* (Ebury Press, 1987) and her *Good Housekeeping vegetarian microwave cookbook* (Ebury Press, 1987), both 128 page paperbacks. *The vegetarian microwave cookbook* by Gail Duff (Windward, 1986) provides recipes for soups and appetisers, snacks, main meals, salads and desserts, with advice and recipes for entertaining. *Microwave Chinese cooking* by Deh-Ta Hsiung (Macdonald Orbis, 1988) makes the most of the microwave's properties to retain flavour, colour, texture and food value in traditional Chinese dishes. Joanna Farrow, *Seafood microwave cookery* (Grub Street, 1987), encourages more adventurous cooking through seafood recipes which can be cooked in minutes. The Good Housekeeping Institute provides a step-by-step guide to *Successful microwave baking* (Ebury Press, 1987) in recipes ranging from basic biscuits to Black Forest gâteau.

Other cooking techniques

Almost every cooking technique in existence has at least one book written about it, and only a few examples are mentioned here. Dianne

Page, *Pressure cooking properly explained* (rev. edn, 1986) and *Slow cooking properly explained* (rev. edn, 1984), are both basic paperbacks from Elliott Right Way Books, giving information on techniques plus a wider range of recipes than is normally provided in the handbook accompanying the cooker. There have been almost as many wok cookbooks published perhaps as there have been woks sold in Britain, but a useful and authentic work is Yong Yap Cotterell, *Wok magic: Chinese cooking for pleasure* (Weidenfeld & Nicolson, 1987), a collection of more than 200 traditional recipes, some of them never previously published in English. *The wok cookbook* by Kenneth Lo (Grafton, 1981) is an excellent paperback introduction, many times reprinted. Cooking at the table is introduced clearly and helpfully in Marion Howells, *Fondue and table top cookery* (Octopus, 1977). There is a wider range of recipes in *The book of fondues* by Lorna Rhodes (Salamander, 1987), including teriyaki, classic cheese and chocolate fondues, and purées of fruit and vegetables. Food processors speed up a lot of standard preparation, but used fully can extend the range of dishes made. Michael Barry, *Food processor cookery* (ICTC, 1983), is published by the distributors of Magimix and Robot Chef equipment, but can be used with any processor. It explains techniques thoroughly, and there is a full range of recipes helpfully illustrated with photographs of the processes. Dianne Page, *Food processors properly explained: with recipes* (Elliott Right Way Books, 1984), is basic and useful. *Get more from your deep fat fryer* by Petra Kühne (Foulsham, 1987) describes this method of cooking and its advantages, then provides recipes for main courses, vegetable and sweet dishes, with ideas for accompanying salads, sauces and dips. *The complete barbecue book* by Jim Marks (Penguin, 1985) is subtitled "everything you need to know about outdoor entertaining", and is a very clear and thorough guide to the equipment, skills and techniques for successful barbecues. It describes the range of different cooking methods, with a good collection of imaginative recipes.

FOOD PRESERVING

Preserving for the long winter months the foods produced in a relatively short growing season is part of traditional British cooking, and though we no longer have the need to preserve meat and fish, the techniques of smoking, curing and drying can still be used to produce well-flavoured foods for special occasions. More commonly, we still preserve fruits and vegetables, by bottling, or as jams, pickles and chutneys, for which there is a section in most general cookery books. Freezing is now a common technique for storing raw or prepared foods.

Maggie Black, *Smoking food at home* (David & Charles, 1985), is mainly about equipment and procedures but contains a number of recipes for using the wide range of smoked foods that can be produced on a domestic scale. Naomi Nichols, *Food drying at home* (David & Charles, 1978), also gives plenty of information on the equipment necessary for home drying – adapting what you already have where possible – and explains methods for drying domestic quantities of fruit and vegetables. There is brief information on fish, meat, poultry and game. A very comprehensive and authoritative work covering a wide range of meat, game, poultry and seafood is Keith Erlandson's *Home smoking and curing* (rev. edn, Hutchinson, 1982). It has a clear explanatory text and helpful illustrations.

All types of preserving are covered thoroughly in the *Good Housekeeping complete book of home preserving* (Ebury Press, 1981). It offers a huge range of recipes for jams, jellies, conserves, pickles, chutneys and sauces; and for the techniques of salting, storing, drying, curing, smoking, candying and crystallising.

Many books confine themselves to fruit and vegetables, and a reliable work is the Ministry of Agriculture, Fisheries and Food's *Home preservation of fruit and vegetables,* a government publication first published in 1929 and now in its thirteenth edition (HMSO, 1971). It covers a wide range of techniques including bottling, canning, freezing, drying and salting, and contains all the basic jam and jelly recipes. All procedures are described in a thorough and practical manner.

One highly specialised book is worth mentioning here: *The book of marmalade: its antecedents, its history and its role in the world today* by C. A. Wilson (Constable, 1985). As well as the nicely illustrated history, the author provides a collection of recipes for marmalade and marmalade cookery.

Freezing is a technique for preserving raw and cooked foods at very low temperatures, and preparation and packing methods are important to achieve success. All aspects of the subject are covered in Jeni Wright's *Complete encyclopaedia of home freezing* (Treasure Press, 1986). For the dedicated food freezer, Pat Cox's *Deep freezing: a comprehensive guide to its theory and practice* (Faber, 1968) is a textbook – though by no means too technical for the amateur cook – with an excellent collection of recipes using to the full the freezer's potential. Last reprinted in 1979, it is no longer in print, but worth seeking out in libraries. The same author has written a briefer book with less theory: *The home book of food freezing* (new edn, Faber, 1977), which is a good beginner's guide. There are numerous "freezer cookbooks" available, yet once the principles of cooking and packing for the freezer are established from books such as those listed above, or even from manuals accompanying home freezers, recipes from any source can be used.

FAST FOOD

In the vocabulary of eating out, "fast food" has a special meaning closely associated with burgers, fries and milk shakes. There are books available on fast food at home however, and they aim to help those who do not like cooking or have not the time for a lot of preparation. In the first category comes Peg Bracken's *Compleat I hate to cook book* (Arlington, 1986). It does not let anyone off cooking, but gives recipes for fast and last-minute meals without complex preparation of either the ingredients or the finished dish. The author is not shy of using pre-prepared, tinned or frozen ingredients, and gives lots of tips for cutting corners or providing quick substitutes for what would otherwise be very time-consuming effects. *Good Housekeeping good food fast* by Susanna Tee (Ebury Press, 1987) is based on fresh foods and offers recipes for one, two or more people which can take from five to forty-five minutes to prepare and cook. There are also prepare-ahead recipes. Hilary Walden in *Cuisine express* (Ward Lock, 1986) grades her recipes for difficulty, time and expense.

Eating raw or pre-cooked foods cuts out cooking altogether, and *Feasting on raw foods,* edited by Charles Gerras (Thorsons, 1986), gives a range of starter, main course, dessert and snack recipes for healthy and quick eating. *No-cook cookery* by Heather Bampfylde and Melanie Faldo (Sackville Books, 1987) also emphasises healthy eating in the recipes provided for fast appetisers, main courses and desserts. Carol Bowen, *No need to cook book* (Hamlyn, 1981), is an attractive collection of recipes using uncooked and ready cooked foods (including meat and fish) in combination to produce soups, main courses, salads and desserts.

Preparation and timing are less of an issue when main course ingredients are all cooked together in one vessel. Gail Duff, *One-pot meals* (Hamlyn, 1987), gives traditional recipes for soups, potato dishes, dumpling and hatted meals, cobblers, pies, and rice and pasta dishes. A complementary selection is available in Jennifer Brennan's *One-dish meals of Asia* (Hale, 1986), which is aimed at the busy cook and includes low-calorie and vegetarian recipes. For rushed vegetarians David Scott has put together *The 30 minute vegetarian: over 200 fast and easy recipes for the healthy cook in a hurry* (Century, 1986). It covers soups and starters, salads and dressings, vegetables and sauces, grains and pasta, pulses, egg, cheese and yoghurt dishes, desserts and fruit dishes.

The classic fast food book, though the title should not be taken too literally if you are thinking of preparing a four-course meal, is Edouard de Pomiane's *Cooking in ten minutes* (Faber, 1985), first published in English in 1948. It is amusing but practical reading.

COOKING ON A BUDGET

Cooking on a low budget does not mean "half-hearted trickery with a tin-opener and a pinch of herbs", says Jocasta Innes in her introduction to *The pauper's cookbook* (Penguin, 1979), but "good, solid rewarding food"; and she provides a collection of economical recipes from European, Chinese and American cuisines, with practical suggestions for menu-planning and shopping, quick meals, and entertaining. *The student's cookbook* by Jenny Baker (Faber, 1985) is a popular basic guide to buying and cooking economically but properly; and Maggie Black, *Healthy eating on a low budget* (Blandford, 1985), provides simple recipes for seasonal fresh foods to give good value-for-money nutrition.

Eatability by Jocasta Innes (Macdonald Orbis, 1987) focuses on entertaining on a budget. *Tante Marie's elegant economic entertaining* (Foulsham, 1986) offers budget menus for lunches and celebration dinners, taking into account quality, nutritional value and presentation. Geraldene Holt's *Budget gourmet* (Hodder & Stoughton, 1984; new edn, Penguin, 1985) does a similar job, but without the advice on menu-planning.

If you are interested in low budget cooking, see also the section on vegetarian cooking in Chapter 6. Vegetarian meals use relatively inexpensive grains, pulses and fresh vegetables, for healthy but economical eating.

FOOD FOR SPECIAL OCCASIONS

Festivals

When life was hard, communities and families saved up preserved foods or money to spend on food so that they could celebrate special occasions with the best of everything. In the western world most of us can eat "festive foods" − turkeys, fruits, puddings and pies, special cakes and sweets − every day if we wish, so that many of the traditional festivals which were excuses for richer food, seasonal food, or just more food than usual, have died out. *Cattern cakes and lace: a calendar of traditional festivals and food* by Julia Jones and Barbara Deer (Dorling 1987) revives traditional British festivals month by month and discusses the folklore, crafts and food associated with them. *The National Trust book of Christmas and festive day recipes* by Sara Paston-Williams (David & Charles, 1981; Penguin, 1983) is a collection of traditional and often forgotten recipes for special meals. Christmas dominates, but Twelfth Night, Midsummer Eve, Michaelmas and the other familiar festivals are well represented. In Britain Christmas is regarded as having had its Golden Age in the Victorian era. Evelyn Dix and Jean Smith in *A Victorian Christmas: traditional recipes for the festive season* (Arlington, 1987) have produced a range of recipes for traditional Christmas dishes, drinks, cakes and preserves, as well as complete menus for Christmas dinner and Boxing Day.

Seasons

Good economical cooking makes use of seasonal fruits, vegetables, meat and fish, and there is something very satisfying about eating the right food at the right time even though modern food preservation methods and transport arrangements ensure that most foods are available all the year round. A number of cookery books do take a seasonal approach. *The cookery year* (Reader's Digest/Hodder & Stoughton, 1973) is now in its fifteenth year; organised by month it lists food in season at the beginning of each section. Recipes are arranged under: soups and starters; fish; meat; poultry and game; rice and pasta; vegetables and salads; sweets and puddings; and all are based on fresh foods in season. Marika Hanbury-Tenison provides a selection of recipes at the end of each section for snacks and savouries from left-overs. There is a substantial introductory section on "Buying for quality" by Zena Skinner, and 100 pages of "Basic cooking methods", contributions on wine and food, planning and equipping a kitchen, and home freezing. It is not an everyday cookbook however; many of the recipes are in the gourmet class either because of the nature of the ingredients or the complex preparation. An inexpensive but less thorough alternative is *The four seasons cookbook* (Marshall Cavendish, 1987), a collection of recipes using seasonal produce.

Daily meals

A number of cookery writers have devoted themselves to the "seasons of the day" and provide recipes for breakfasts and teas particularly, probably because lunches and dinners are well catered for in the main course sections of other cookery books. *The breakfast book* by Diana Troy (Allison & Busby, 1985) contains a wide range of traditional and unexpected recipes under the headings: bread and butter; oatcakes; scones; cereals; pancakes and fritters; eggs; hearty breakfasts; vegetables; fish; summer breakfasts; jams; festive breakfasts. It is a book sufficiently interesting to encourage even coffee-and-a-cigarette breakfasters to reconsider. Jennie Reekie's *Little breakfast book* (Piatkus, 1987), like fellow members of the Little Book series, is a collection of facts, tips and quotations about breakfast as well as recipes.

The number of books on the subject would suggest that the traditional English tea is being revived. Michael Smith's *Afternoon tea* (Macmillan, 1986) is the most substantial work on offer, and provides a short history of the social background and significance of afternoon tea, as well as a collection of traditional, new and regional recipes for sandwiches and fillings; jams and chutneys; crumpets; scones; bread and rolls; cakes; cheesecakes and biscuits. Jane Pettigrew, *Tea time* (Dorling Kinderlsey, 1986), is a collection of regional and traditional tea-time recipes with a number of new ones developed by the author. Two books are arranged around complete tea-time menus. Joanna Isles, *A proper tea: an English collection of recipes* (Piatkus, 1987), features eleven teas including a farmhouse tea and tea in the garden, with 50 recipes. *Having tea* by Tricia Foley (Sidgwick & Jackson, 1987) is a collection of 14 tea-time menus and settings, with 50 recipes including tarts, pies and cream cakes. *The London Ritz book of afternoon tea* (Ebury Press, 1986) examines the art and pleasures of taking tea, and provides ideas and recipes.

All the above books are glossy, spacious, well-illustrated and produced, nice to own, but most suitable perhaps for the gift book market since the recipes are readily available in more general cookbooks.

Many of the books discussed in the section on Entertaining also cover food and menu-planning for special occasions.

ENTERTAINING

Though many general cookery books contain menus and recipes for entertaining (*The cookery year,* for example, covers wedding receptions and celebration dinner parties), those specialising in entertaining recognise the additional importance of forward planning, timing, presentation and atmosphere. Jan Hopcraft, *Cooking today – eating tomorrow* (Eyre Methuen, 1972), provides menus and recipes for a range of occasions such as an organised dinner or lunch; a fork supper; the unexpected guest; and food to eat with drinks. The emphasis, as the title suggests, is on advance preparation and cooking. Dinner parties are the theme of a number of books. *The Good Food Guide dinner party book* by Hilary Fawcett and Jeanne Strang (Consumers' Association/Hodder & Stoughton, 1971) provides seasonal menus for gourmet cooking. Alexandra Carlier, *The dinner party book: planned menus for busy gourmets* (Collins, 1986), is aimed at those with a tight work schedule. There are 24 menus with recipes emphasising well-balanced food and the correct progression of wines, with a detailed work schedule for each. The food is largely French cuisine. Dinner party themes and recipes from around the world feature in *The international dinner party cookbook* by Jan Bilton (Piatkus, 1986), and quantities are for four to fifty people.

Not all entertaining is formal, and Sophie Grigson's *Food for friends* (Ebury Press, 1987) provides ideas for entertaining using recipes which adapt to ordinary family cooking methods. Jeni Wright, *Entertaining with friends* (Ebury Press, 1987), though it does not ignore the importance of atmosphere created by settings, table decoration and lighting, provides hospitable recipes for a range of informal occasions such as late breakfasts and midsummer parties. Prue Leith and Polly Tyrer make an art of creating party atmosphere in *Entertaining with style* (Macdonald, 1986), with over 200 recipes plus party ideas and practical information for planning a party. Themes for food and atmosphere include a Burns Night dinner and a Surrealist dinner. The attention to detail demanded of users of this book requires total dedication and enthusiasm!

Most of the recipe books specialising in cooking for guests do provide recipes for rich foods on the assumption that you will probably spend more money and forget your diet on special occasions. However Evelyn Findlater has produced a book to suit vegetarians, vegans *or* meat-eaters. Called *The natural entertainer: the healthy way to delicious food* (Century, 1987), it adapts recipes for a range of eating styles, reflects the cuisines of many countries, but above all concentrates on healthy foods.

Not all cookery writers provide information about wine with meals, though this is a particularly important aspect of entertaining. A useful book to accompany the menu-planners therefore is Jancis Robinson's *Food and wine adventures* (Headline Books, 1987) (Figure 5.2). It is not a manual or chart, but an informal description of traditional and more unexpected combinations of wine with food, and at a range of prices. It should encourage experimentation. The author is well known for her television wine programmes.

Books in the section "Cooking on a budget" (above) contain recipes and menu suggestions for entertaining economically.

FOOD AS PRESENTS

There are many ideas and recipes for food as presents in many of the books discussed elsewhere in this chapter, particularly cakes, biscuits, sweets and chocolates, jams, conserves, pickles and chutneys. However there are some imaginative books dealing specifically with this topic. Annette Grimsdale, *The book of gifts from the pantry* (Salamander, 1986), is a clearly presented little book, simply laid out with a recipe per page, and a colour photograph at each stage of preparation. It covers sauces; sweet and savoury preserves; snacks; drinks; sweets; baked be said that no one could be working harder to counteract this somewhat blimpish reaction than the top Rheingau producers themselves.

Vive les blancs! Though remember that most whites up to the job of accompanying a main course will have sufficient extract that they shouldn't be left in the fridge or ice bucket too long.

CHAPTER TWENTY
GOOD, PLAIN FOOD
WHAT WE REALLY EAT
'[Wine] awakens and refreshes the lurking passions of the mind, as varnish does the colours which are sunk in a picture, and brings them out in all their natural glowings.' ALEXANDER POPE

So far, you might be forgiven for thinking that my diet was one long succession of dishes *de luxe*: a *langouste* here, a slice of *foie gras* there, not *another* three-star restaurant this evening.

My life is not like that actually — nor, I suspect, is yours. In fact, thanks to the work of Mr John Squire Kirkham of the London Clinic on my loved one's stomach, the food I eat at home is probably considerably plainer, and certainly more meat-dominated, than the national average.

I reckon I'm pretty well qualified therefore to recommend wines to go with such staples as sausages and shepherd's pie. In our household we drink wine every night, and see no contradiction, only elevation, in matching exotic foreign liquids with stolid domestic solids. I must admit though, that in a more temperate or economical household, a glass of water or even a cup of tea would go really rather well with many British basics.

It is difficult to make blanket recommendations since these basics vary so much in flavour and intensity, but here are a few of the distinctly less adventurous main dishes (some distinctly un-British) served *chez* Lander with wines we've found to be particularly successful.

Bacon: Is it because I know they're 'difficult' with wine that I've convinced myself I don't like fried eggs? (See next chapter.) Anyway, I can strongly recommend bacon as a good excuse for drinking one of the many slightly sweet-tasting young light- to medium-bodied reds that are made in Cal-

Figure 5.2   Wine with meals: an informal description

ifornia, Australia and Spain. It's the familiar sweet and salt principle that makes this combination work, but the wines need to be frank and fruity, as opposed to complex and mature, to meet something as humble as bacon on its own ground.

Beef Stroganoff: I like the formulation of spices and seasonings prescribed by the *Silver Palate Cookbook* — lots of everything from Hungarian paprika thru', as they would doubtless say, Dijon mustard to Worcestershire sauce. This means that only a fairly fiery wine need apply for the post of glass-filling with my Stroganoff. I find southern Rhône reds, such as Châteauneuf-du-Pape, Gigondas, Vacqueyras and top quality Côtes-du-Rhône of the Château de Fonsalette sort do the job extremely well thanks to their similar make-up of different flavours and considerable weight through sheer force of alcohol level. The purist in me searches in vain for a really robust red exported from Hungary, but Bulgaria (not the same thing at all, I do realize) can certainly oblige — notably with the powerful indigenous grapes Mavrud and, even more concentrated, Melnik.

Calves' liver: This popular source of protein and iron, so much more satisfying cut thicker than the restaurant norm, tastes notably sweet for a meat. As with its relative, *foie gras*, it is easy to make a sickly combination by drinking too sweet a wine with it.

Source: Jancis Robinson, *Food and wine adventures* (Headline, 1987), pp. 64-5. © Jancis Robinson 1987; illus. © John Lawrence 1987. Reproduced by kind permission of Headline Book Publishing plc.

items; and suggestions for gift assortments. Though the illustrations give some ideas these are incidental, and more positive information on boxing and wrapping would complete an otherwise useful book. Sally Taylor, *Gourmet gifts* (Windward, 1986), is helpful on packaging and presentation, and concentrates on preserves and traditional sweets and chocolates. *Harrods book of chocolates and other edible gifts* (Ebury Press, 1986) has a good range of sweet recipes from fondant to mint humbugs, butterscotch to candied fruits. Edible gifts including jams and preserves, chocolates, mueslis and healthy snacks, drinks and sweets, are a substantial part of a wider ranging crafts book by Kay Fairfax called *Homemade* (Dryad, 1986).

THE YOUNG COOK

Many of the cookery books for children put too much emphasis on sweet and junk foods — presumably to attract young buyers; a perfectly respectable fresh fruit salad in one work is marred by the addition of marshmallows, for example. Other cookery writers feel that healthy food and children are not incompatible. Peggy Brusseau's *Let's cook it together* (Thorsons, 1986) is subtitled "Utterly scrumptious recipes for you and your children — to make together — vegetarian style". There are recipes for soups, salads, rice and pasta, flans, baking, cooker top meals, snacks, treats and drinks. It is a large format paperback, beautifully set out in step-by-step style. Evelyn Findlater, *Full of beans: super healthy recipes for kids to cook themselves* (Thorsons, 1987), is also a meatless cookbook, with clear and easy-to-follow layout and attractive illustrations. *The kitchen crew: a children's wholefood cookery book* by Stephanie Lashford (Ashgrove Press, 1987) is informative, clear and worthwhile. There are three volumes in the Usborne First Cookbooks series: *Hot things* (1983): *Party things* (1984); and *Sweet things* (1987), all by Angela Wilkes and Stephen Cartwright. They are not quite so "healthy", and the illustrated strip recipes, though attractive to adult eyes, are perhaps a little messy for children to follow easily — depending on age. Bridget Jones, *High-speed food: microwave meals and snacks for young cooks* (Hamlyn, 1987), provides recipes for main meals; vegetarian dishes; suppers; snacks; puddings and sweets; and is aimed at teenagers rather than younger children. There is perhaps too much emphasis on the use of canned, frozen and packet foods, but the recipes are mostly nutritious and healthy, and designed to be attractive to the age group.

Specifically for handicapped children, James Hargreaves, *Cookery for handicapped people* (Souvenir Press, 1986), provides recipes with a minimum of words, using sequential drawings instead. An introductory section gives advice for parents and teachers on equipment, and the skills the child needs to develop.

REGIONAL COOKING

Britain

Though British cooking is the butt of jokes at home and abroad, in fact home cooking well done has developed over the centuries to make the best use of a wide range of high-quality indigenous meats, fish, vegetables and grain. It is true that British cookery does not have a classic literature to the extent that French cooking has; the names Eliza Acton and Hannah Glasse may be well known to cookery enthusiasts, but it was really only with Eliza Beeton in the nineteenth century that a household name in cooking emerged. *Mrs Beeton's cookery and household management* was sufficiently successful to have merited reprints to the present day. Facsimiles of the 1861 edition are available (Cape, 1968; Chancellor, 1983). There is also a revised edition published by Ward Lock (1980) which is metricated and illustrated with colour photographs (all of which seems to go against the spirit of the work); and *The shorter Mrs Beeton* (Ward Lock, 1987) with 400 recipes and new photographs. There are a number of overviews of cooking in the British Isles. Probably the most authoritative is *British cookery: a complete guide to culinary practice in the British Isles,* edited by Lizzie Boyd (Croom Helm/British Farm Produce Council/British Tourist Authority, 1976). It provides a brief history of British cooking and an outline of cookery methods in 100 pages; over 400 pages of recipes all stating area of origin; an essay entitled "A scientific approach to professional cookery"; a glossary and a bibliography. It is a reference tool rather than a heavily illustrated coffee-table book, but is a most comprehensive anthology of regional British recipes. *The Observer guide to British cookery* (Michael Joseph, 1984; paperback edn, Michael Joseph, 1986) is arranged by region and is a visually attractive illustrated overview of British regional food and recipes. It covers the south-west, London and the south, the Midlands, East Anglia, the north-east, the north-west, Scotland, Wales and Ireland. There is an excellent bibliography and a hotel and restaurant guide which will of course have a limited lifespan. Marika Hanbury Tenison, *The best of British cooking* (Hart-Davis/MacGibbon, 1976), though now out of print, is worth trying to get hold of, being a very good collection of "homely" recipes using local ingredients and covering all centuries, though without any indication of region of origin. *A cook's tour of Britain* prepared by the Women's Institute and Michael Smith (Willow Books, 1984) is arranged by region, with recipes that have adapted themselves to ingredients available throughout the United Kingdom. The book is clearly set out, and is essentially a recipe book without a great deal of historic and supplementary information.

As well as overviews of British cooking, there are books focusing on food in the four kingdoms and areas within them. Examples of these are examined below; literary warrant rather than overt racism requires that Scotland, Ireland and Wales are discussed under one heading.

England

Jane Grigson's *English food* (new edn, Penguin, 1986) is a collection of traditional English and Welsh (despite the title) recipes for soups; vegetables; fish; meat; poultry and game; cheese and eggs; baking; sauces and preserves. Jane Grigson writes informally and informatively on the sources of the recipes, the ingredients and preparation methods. Many recipes use foods that tend to be neglected now – herrings, brains, eels, sorrel. A similar work, but with an emphasis on north country recipes, is Peggy Hutchinson, *Old English cookery* (Foulsham, 1973). Susan Campbell, *English cookery new and old* (Consumers' Association/Hodder & Stoughton, 1981), is arranged by season, and under rather whimsical headings such as "Breakfast for a long day ahead" and "A game dinner in the North", but is useful in providing menu ideas on a theme, often regional, and adapts old recipes to modern cooking methods. Michael Smith, *New English cookery* (BBC, 1985), uses the traditional ingredients of English cooking, but in new combinations. The pie is a traditional and much-loved food featured in all the books mentioned so far, and Sara Paston-Williams, *The National Trust book of pies* (David & Charles, 1987), concentrates on the English pie, from the highly spiced and sweetened pies served at medieval banquets to the twentieth-century home-baked pie.

Narrower regions within England are given special treatment by some writers. Marika Hanbury Tenison's *Recipes from a country kitchen* (Granada, 1978) is a book of West Country food compiled from personal sources and old manuscripts. Theodora Fitzgibbon, *Traditional West Country cookery* (Fontana, 1982), is a substantial collection of recipes, many of them from within the experience of the author's family. In the same author's "A taste of . . ." series published by Pan are recipe books covering the West Country (1975); London (1987); Yorkshire (1979); the Lake District (1980); and England (1986). Each paperback is a collection of traditional recipes and historical photographs of the area. Peter Brears, *Traditional food in Yorkshire* (Edinburgh: John Macdonald, 1984), is "an accurate study of the food and drink prepared and eaten in ordinary Yorkshire houses during the nineteenth century". Eating habits are placed in the context of work and environment, so it is a social history, but with many usable recipes: porridge and oatcakes have a chapter each! Hilary Whitbread, *A year in a Yorkshire kitchen* (Dalesman, 1988), is arranged by month, and is more of a conventional recipe book than Brears, but includes information on special days and customs. Sheila Hutchins, *Grannie's kitchen: the north-east* (Granada, 1979), is a collection of recipes from the whole of the north of England and not the narrow region stated in the title. That quibble apart, it is worth trying to get hold of because many of the recipes come from old hand-written family cookbooks and personal sources, and were previously unpublished. There are many regional cookbooks published and/or distributed by local history groups, library and museum services and tourist boards, and these are worth looking out for in local bookshops and other organisations.

The Celtic countries

Iris Price Jones, *Celtic cookery* (2nd rev. edn, Swansea: Christopher Davies, 1984) is an interesting concept. In sections covering Brittany, Cornwall, Ireland, the Isle of Man, Scotland and Wales, the book provides recipes for soups, savouries, puddings, baking, fish, meat, poultry and game, and shows some of the similarities in the traditional dishes of these countries and regions. Most other cookery books in this field concentrate on food and cooking in either Scotland, Ireland or

Wales, and coverage of Cornwall and the Isle of Man is left to some of the general works on British cooking.

A classic Scottish text is *The Scots kitchen: its traditions and lore with old-time recipes* (2nd edn, Blackie, 1963; new edn, Mayflower, 1974). It is not a "complete compendium of Scottish cookery" but a document to preserve from extinction the recipes of old national dishes — particularly folk recipes. When it was first published in 1929 many of the recipes had never before been published. For modern readers some of them will have no more than a historic interest, but overall it is a fascinating work with descriptions of the larder, the table and menus, the kitchen, and traditional hospitality. There are many modern books of interest to the contemporary cook. Catherine Brown, *Scottish regional recipes* (new edn, Penguin, 1983), is divided into 10 regional sections such as Edinburgh and the Lothians, and Dumfries and Galloway, with a sample of traditional recipes in each. Theodora Fitzgibbon, *A taste of Scotland* (Pan, 1971), is in the series format of pages of traditional recipes faced by old photographs. A good standard work is A. King and F. Dunnett, *The home book of Scottish cookery* (Faber, 1973). Worth a special mention is its straightforward and manageable recipe for haggis, actually a "pot" or "pan" haggis which does not require the stomach bag or pluck. Game is part of traditional Scottish diets, and Julia Drysdale, *Classic game cookery* (Papermac, 1983); and Nichola Fletcher, *Game for all, with a flavour of Scotland* (Gollancz, 1987), are thorough and useful books. The latter is a collection of more unusual recipes.

Traditional Irish cooking is covered by a number of works including Theodora Fitzgibbon, *A taste of Ireland* (Pan, 1970); the same author's *Irish traditional food* (Macmillan, 1983; Pan, 1984); and George L. Thomson, *Traditional Irish recipes* (2nd rev. edn, Dublin: O'Brien Press, 1986). Rosie Tinne's *Irish country house cooking* (Gill and Macmillan, 1974), though now out of print, emphasises gourmet foods to counteract the stereotype of traditional Irish "cottage" or "peasant" cooking. It is an interesting collection of recipes contributed by the owners of country houses.

Welsh cooking is also represented by Theodora Fitzgibbon in *A taste of Wales* (Pan, 1973), a useful introduction to traditional recipes. More thorough is Bobby Freeman, *Book of Welsh food: "First catch your peacock"* (Image Imprint, 1980). As already mentioned in the section on England, Jane Grigson's *English food* (new edn, Penguin, 1986) provides a full range of recipes from traditional Welsh cuisine.

World regional cookery

The quantity of books available in this country on world national cuisines is too vast to discuss in any systematic and thorough way, so this section is limited to the description of a sample of works for a sample of countries, regions or continents. Hopefully they are books which give a good introduction to the authentic ingredients, recipes and presentation of each cuisine.

One series of books now out of print, but worth consulting if the individual volumes can be tracked down in libraries or second-hand bookshops, is the "Time-Life Foods of the World" series published during the late 1960s and early 1970s. Each work consists of a hardback book on the environment, culture and food of the region, heavily illustrated and with some recipes, and a separate spiral-bound recipe booklet, both contained in a white plastic pictorial binder. Titles are *The cooking of the British Isles; Germany; India; Italy; Japan; The Middle East; Russia; Scandinavia; Spain and Portugal; Vienna's Empire; Classic French cooking; American cooking; Latin American cooking;* and *A quintet of cuisines* covering Switzerland, the Low Countries, Poland, Bulgaria and Romania, and North Africa. They are excellent introductory works. An American series, *Cooking the . . . way,* is published by Lerner Publications Co. and is available in Great Britain: in print at the time of writing (April 1988) are the African, Caribbean, Chinese, English, French, German, Greek, Hungarian, Indian, Israeli, Italian, Japanese, Korean, Lebanese, Mexican, Norwegian, Polish, Russian, Spanish, Thai and Vietnamese volumes.

Europe and the Mediterranean

A general book on European food is Elisabeth Luard, *European peasant cookery: the rich tradition* (Bantam, 1986), a substantial collection of down-to-earth filling recipes using meat, game, pulses, root vegetables, berries, nuts and grains. Each chapter deals with a single basic ingredient; in the meat chapter there are recipes for reindeer but not wild boar. The book is an interesting read as well as an excellent collection of recipes.

Cakes and pastries are some of the characteristic foods of Germany and Austria, and Sarah Kelly's *Festive baking in Austria, Germany and Switzerland* (Penguin, 1985) covers Lebkuchen, egg and butter baking, yeast dumplings and fruit breads, cakes and pastries. Josephine Bacon, *Patisserie of Vienna* (Macdonald Orbis, 1988), provides a further eighty recipes for confections ranging from the easy to the elaborate. A more general introduction to German food is Hanne Lambley, *The home book of German cookery* (Faber, 1979). It provides standard and regional recipes in the basic format of this series. Eva M. Borer, *Tante Heidi's Swiss kitchen* (Kaye & Ward, 1965), is a basic introduction to Swiss dishes, containing many cheese recipes and a healthy eating section.

Classic English works on French cooking are Elizabeth David's *French country cooking* and *French provincial cooking*. The former was first published in 1951 and is now available in a new illustrated edition from Dorling Kindersley (1987). Said the *Observer* of *French provincial cooking* (Michael Joseph, 1960), "one could cook for a lifetime on this book alone". It is a substantial book giving a flavour of the region, its history and the characteristic ingredients; both works provide a collection of authentic recipes, lovingly decribed. A more recent work is *La cuisine: the complete book of French cooking* (Macdonald Orbis, 1987), first published in France in 1980. It is a large format work with helpful sections on equipment and cooking method, and hundreds of clearly set out and well-illustrated recipes which are graded (by number of chef's hats!) to indicate level of difficulty (Figure 5.3) Classic French recipes are selected by a popular French cookery writer in *Francoise Bernard's French cooking* (Macdonald Orbis, 1987); it contains 256 illustrated recipes. Regional cooking is covered in a range of works of which a recent example is Paula Wolfert, *The cooking of South West France* (Dorling Kindersley, 1987), which examines the gastronomy of the region between Perigord and the Pyrenees exemplified in 150 recipes.

A thorough and substantial work on Italian cooking is *The Italian cookery book* compiled by the Italian Academy of Cookery (Pelham, 1987). It covers traditional, classic and regional foods, and though the illustrations are mainly decorative, the book is highly practical. It is arranged primarily by ingredient (meat, poultry, pasta, and so on) and instructions are clear and well set out. Another attractive and useful compendium is *La cucina: the complete book of Italian cooking* (Macdonald Orbis, 1987), a companion to *La cuisine* mentioned above.

Polenta

	00:05	00:30 to 01:00

American	Ingredients	Metric/Imperial
1 quart	Water	1 l / 1¾ pints
2 tsp	Salt	2 tsp
8 oz	Coarse yellow corn meal [polenta]	225 g / 8 oz

1. Bring the water and the salt to a rapid boil. Sprinkle in the corn meal very slowly, stirring all the time with a wooden spoon.
2. When the mixture is thick and smooth, cover the pan and lower the heat. Cook for 30-40 minutes or until the corn meal is coming away from the sides of the saucepan.
3. Polenta can be served soft and very hot, like a purée, accompanied by various garnishes, or with butter and parmesan cheese. Or leave the prepared polenta to cool on a board and it can then be reheated in a variety of ways. Cut into squares, cover with tomato or other sauce and bake in a moderate oven; fry until golden in oil and butter; or try polenta fritters – coated in egg and bread crumbs and deep-fried.

Penne à la diable

Penne with Bacon and Mushroom Sauce

	00:30	00:45

American	Ingredients	Metric/Imperial
¾ lb	Button mushrooms	350 g / 12 oz
6 oz	Bacon	175 g / 6 oz
1 lb	Tomatoes	500 g / 1 lb
1	Fresh basil sprig	1
½	Sweet green or red pepper	½
2	Garlic cloves	2
6 tbsp	Butter	75 g / 3 oz
	Salt and pepper	
1 lb	Penne	500 g / 1 lb
¾ cup	Grated parmesan cheese	75 g / 3 oz

1. Clean the mushrooms and cut into thin slices. Cut the bacon into small strips. Peel the tomatoes (first plunging them into boiling water for 10 seconds) and cut in half. Remove the seeds and chop coarsely. Chop the basil leaves. Remove the seeds and white parts of the pepper and cut the flesh into very thin strips. Peel and crush the garlic.
2. Heat half the butter in a frying pan and brown the bacon for about 5 minutes. Remove with a slotted spoon and set aside.
3. Add the mushrooms to the same pan and cook for 10 minutes or until all the liquid has evaporated. Remove with a slotted spoon and place on one side.
4. Add the pepper and crushed garlic to the pan, cook for 2-3 minutes and then remove with a slotted spoon.
5. Place the tomatoes in the pan, season with salt and pepper and cook over a moderate heat for 20 minutes, stirring from time to time.
6. Return the bacon, mushrooms, pepper and garlic to the pan and add the chopped basil. Keep warm over a low heat.
7. Boil a large cooking pot of salted water and add the penne. Bring back to a boil and cook for about 10 minutes or until 'al

dente' (see page 437). Drain well and place in a warmed serving dish. Sprinkle with the parmesan cheese and dot with the remaining butter. Finally, pour over the sauce and toss just before serving.

Tagliatelle aux cèpes

Tagliatelle with Cèpes

	00:15	00:25

American	Ingredients	Metric/Imperial
1 lb	Fresh cèpes or other mushrooms	500 g / 1 lb
2	Garlic cloves	2
¼ cup	Olive oil	4 tbsp
	Salt and pepper	
1 tbsp	Chopped fresh parsley	1 tbsp
¼ cup	Crème fraîche (see page 122)	4 tbsp
1 lb	Tagliatelle	500 g / 1 lb
½ cup	Grated parmesan cheese	50 g / 2 oz

1. Clean and trim the mushrooms and cut into thin slices. Peel and chop the garlic cloves.
2. Heat the olive oil in a frying pan and cook the mushrooms over a low heat. Season with salt and pepper and add the garlic and the chopped parsley. Cook until all the liquid from the mushrooms has evaporated. Stir in the crème fraîche. Remove from the heat and keep hot.
3. Boil a large cooking pot of salted water. Add the tagliatelle and boil for 5-8 minutes if the pasta is fresh, 10-12 minutes if dried. Drain well and toss with the sauce over a gentle heat.
4. To serve, sprinkle with the grated parmesan cheese.

Macaroni au gratin

Macaroni Cheese

	00:20	00:20 to 00:25

American	Ingredients	Metric/Imperial
	Salt and pepper	
1 tbsp	Oil	1 tbsp
1 lb	Macaroni	500 g / 1 lb
⅔ cup	Crème fraîche (see page 122)	150 ml / ¼ pint
2 cups	Grated gruyère cheese	250 g / 8 oz
	Grated nutmeg	
¼ cup	Butter	50 g / 2 oz

1. Bring to a boil a large quantity of salted water in a cooking pot. Add the oil and the macaroni and cook for about 10 minutes or until 'al dente' (see page 437). Drain well.
2. Preheat the oven to 400°F / 200°C / Gas Mark 6
3. Put the macaroni in a large saucepan, add the crème fraîche and cook for 6 minutes, stirring from time to time. Remove from the heat and add two-thirds of the grated cheese, salt, if necessary, pepper and a little freshly grated nutmeg. Mix together and place in a gratin dish. Sprinkle with the remaining grated cheese and dot with the butter
4. Bake for 20-25 minutes until the top is golden brown.

Figure 5.3 Clearly set out and well-illustrated recipes

Source: La cuisine: the complete book of French cooking (Macdonald Orbis, 1987), p. 440. Reproduced by kind permission of Macdonald & Co. (Publishers) Ltd.

It contains over 1000 recipes from the classic Italian cookery book *La pentola d'oro* and covers the full range of ingredients and dishes. Elizabeth David, *Italian food,* first published in 1954, is issued in a revised and illustrated edition by Barrie & Jenkins (1987), and is extremely beautiful visually. The author distinguishes between Florentine, Venetian, Roman, Neopolitan, Umbrian and other regional cuisines, and provides introductory information on Italian kitchens, cooking equipment and basic ingredients. Home baking is the subject of the much more specialised *Patisserie of Italy* by Jeni Wright (Macdonald Orbis, 1988) which provides recipes for biscuits, tarts, sweet breads and gâteaus.

Victoria Serra, *Tia Victoria's Spanish kitchen* (Kaye & Ward, 1963), is a classic cookery book in Spain, and is here adapted to suit British requirements. It provides recipes for all meals, and is a useful introduction. *The Spanish table* by Marimar Torres (Ebury, 1987) is a collection of over 200 recipes for traditional regional dishes, with detailed information on the wine-producing areas and best restaurants of Spain. Tapas, the highly varied "snacks and nibbles" of Spain, are becoming increasingly popular in Britain and America, but are not always authentic or as sophisticated as they are in their native country. Penelope Casas, *Tapas: the little dishes of Spain* (Pavilion Books, 1987), provides a collection of characteristic recipes for appetisers based on seafoods, salads, spiced meats and marinades.

Jean Anderson, *The food of Portugal* (Robert Hale, 1987), is a substantial guide to that country's eating tastes; recipes range from classic soups and the very varied fish dishes to characteristic sweets and desserts. It becomes more than a recipe book by the addition of 35 colour photographs of regional landscapes, which probably make this a more expensive book than it need be for those who would simply like to experiment with a neglected cuisine.

Rena Salaman, *Greek food* (Fontana, 1983), is a helpful, basic, unillustrated introduction to the full range of classic Greek food with background information on the place and the people. It covers appetisers, soups and pulses, stuffed vegetables, olive trees and olive oil, salads, vegetables, pies, poultry and game, fish and meat. The same author's *Greek island cookery* (Ebury, 1987) is a rather more sumptuous production with watercolours. Festival recipes are included in the range offered by Pamela Westland in her *Greek cooking* (Ward Lock, 1987).

Authentic traditional Turkish recipes are provided in a practical format by Arto der Haroutunian in *A Turkish cookbook* (Ebury, 1987).

The countries bordering the Mediterranean have a range of ingredients and cooking and preparation methods that give the food of the whole area a characteristic and distinctive flavour and texture. Elizabeth David captured this well in her *Book of Mediterranean food* (2nd edn, Penguin, 1965), where the atmosphere lies as much in the descriptions of foods as in the recipes. Claudia Roden has become an acknowledged expert on Mediterranean food, and her most recent publication is *Mediterranean cookery* (BBC, 1987) based on her television series. The book contains an excellent range of clearly set out recipes with helpful and attractive illustrations. There is an alphabetical introductory section describing the major ingredients, and an outline of Mediterranean cuisine. Fish and shellfish are heavily used in this region, and Alan Davidson provides regional recipes in his *Mediterranean seafood* (2nd edn, Allen Lane, 1981). It is a practical and reliable guide with a descriptive catalogue of fish. For non-meat eaters, Colin Spencer's *Mediterranean vegetarian cooking* (Thorsons, 1986) concentrates on vegetable and pulse dishes using traditional recipes slightly adapted by the author.

The Soviet Union has absorbed so many cultures that its culinary heritage and repertoire is vast and varied. The food of Russia is essentially "European" however, and an excellent introduction is *The food and cooking of Russia* by Lesley Chamberlain (Allen Lane, 1982). The author sampled home and hotel cooking during a year's stay and compared it with nineteenth-century cuisine. As well as recipes there is information on the history of Russian food, meals and meal times, menu planning, and special ingredients; and the book does touch on other areas of the Soviet Union. For the sake of authenticity ingredients are used that are not necessarily available in this country (for example the hazelhen), but frequently alternatives are suggested. It is a thoroughly "good read" and the recipes (which are organised by principal ingredient) are clearly set out and described. Nina Petrova, *The best of Russian cookery* (Batsford, 1979), is a clear basic compilation of over 350 recipes from Russia and the Ukraine, organised by main ingredient. Darra Goldstein, *A taste of Russia* (Norman/Hale, 1985), has good recipes but is rather idiosyncratically organised under headings such as Zakuska tables; classic recipes; a holiday celebration at the dacha, and so on. Caucasian cuisine (from Armenia, Azerbaidzhan and Georgia) is quite specialised, with overtones of Persian, Arab and Turkish cooking, and over 250 recipes are provided in Sonia Uvezian, *The best foods of Russia* (Harcourt Brace Jovanovich, 1976).

The Balkan cookbook by Vladimir Mirodan (Lennard, 1987) offers recipes characteristic of the Balkan countries whose cuisine is an amalgam of Russian, Eastern and French influences. It is a badly-produced book with unpleasant heavy black type and poorly reproduced illustrations, but is comprehensive with 200 recipes covering all types of dishes, and sections on where to obtain the ingredients and on Balkan wines and spirits.

North and South America and the Caribbean

Traditional North American food is celebrated in *The great illustrated American cookbook* (Dorling Kindersley, 1987), a collection of over 600 recipes including the well-known chicken à la king, southern fried chicken, American apple pie, baked beans, and pumpkin pie. There are step-by-step illustrations (2452 of them) in the text and a separate section of colour photographs. The book has been economically produced and is not particularly attractive to look at, but is a substantial and basic introduction. Complementing this is *The all-American cookbook: America's favourite dishes for non-American cooks* (Piatkus, 1981), with recipes from all over the USA. Regional specialities are covered by Kenna Lach Bifani and Miranda Whyte in *American home cooking: favourite recipes from all over USA* (Macdonald Orbis, 1987); it includes Tex-Mex, Creole and Cajun, and Pacific coast seafood dishes. It is illustrated with 40 aesthetically-pleasing rather than informative colour plates. Alan Davidson again turns his attention to fish in *North Atlantic seafood* (Penguin, 1980), providing a detailed catalogue of fish, and recipes from countries bordering the North Atlantic.

An overview of cooking in South America is provided by *The book of Latin American cooking* by Elisabeth L. Ortiz (Norman/Hale, 1984), and is complemented by a number of more specialised works, for example Carolyn Dehnel, *Mexican cooking* (Ward Lock, 1986), which provides recipes for traditional dishes but with an emphasis on high-fibre and high-protein meals using low-cholesterol fish and poultry.

Floella Benjamin's Caribbean cookery (Rider, 1986) is a good paperback collection of manageable recipes for the full range of foods and includes vegetarian recipes. It is a basic, nicely-presented book, informally and informatively written. Judy Bastyra's *Caribbean cooking* (Windward, 1987) is also a good introduction to the use of the regional fish, shellfish, fruit and vegetables, with 70 colour photographs.

Africa

Most of the readily available books on African cooking are about North Africa, so the recipes share many of the characteristics of those from the northern shores of the Mediterranean. Arto der Haroutunian's *North African cookery* (Century, 1985) claims to be the "first-ever comprehensive" work on this area, and is an excellent introduction to the ingredients, traditional dishes and general eating style. Robert Carrier, *Taste of Morocco* (Century, 1987), with its landscape format and 100 colour photographs, does not look as though it should be allowed to lie around the kitchen, though it does provide more than 150 recipes along with information on how Moroccans shop, prepare their food and eat it. David Scott, *Traditional Arab cookery* (Rider, 1983), is a clear, basic and inexpensive guide to Arab dishes. Moving to more southern regions, *The Africa News cookbook: African cooking for western kitchens,* edited by Tami Hultman (Penguin, 1986), pulls together a wide range of recipes adapted for our cooking methods and the availability of ingredients. A wide variety of recipes from the whole of Nigeria can be found in the *Nigerian cookbook* by H. O. Anthonio and M. Isoun (Macmillan, 1982). It is totally authentic, so that the British user might have to search for some of the ingredients, but is an exciting and properly representative collection.

Asia

The Asian cuisines most familiar to westerners, mainly through restaurants whose popularity has then stimulated books and television programmes, are the Indian and Chinese, but there is increasing interest in the food and meals of other Asian countries. *The best of Asian cooking* by John Mitchell (New Orchard, 1986) provides an overview of fourteen countries in a collection of recipes for starters, seafood, poultry, meat, vegetables and salads, breads, rice and noodles, and desserts. A much more substantial volume (456 pages and 260 illustrations) is *A taste of the Orient* (Macdonald Orbis, 1987) which offers recipes from China, Indonesia, Singapore, Vietnam, Sri Lanka, the Philippines, Burma, Thailand, Korea, Malaysia, India, Pakistan and Japan. More than just a recipe book, it has sections on cooking techniques and equipment, and the preparation of the very important garnishes.

A sound introduction to Indian food is *The home book of Indian cookery* by Sipra Das Gupta (Faber, 1973; Faber paperback, 1980). There is an excellent introduction, and the recipes are then very clearly set out and described in detail, even to the utensils required for each dish. Recipes are arranged by principal ingredient. Madhur Jaffrey is now famous following her television broadcasts, and her books are also clear guides to the art of Indian cooking. *A taste of India* (Pavilion/Michael Joseph, 1985) is more than a recipe book however. Arranged by region, it gives information on the place itself, and on the origins of the traditional local foods. Yamuna Devi, *Lord Krishna's cuisine: the art of Indian vegetarian cooking* (Angus & Robertson, 1987), is a huge book — 800 pages — and covers every type of food in hundreds of recipes. In the introduction to each of the many sections (rice; dals; breads; salads; vegetables; and so on) the author emphasises the spiritual element of food preparation, cooking and eating. Julie Sahni's *Classic Indian vegetarian cooking* (Dorling Kindersley, 1987) also covers the principles of eating as well as recipes, and explains food combinations, the planning and serving of meals, and appropriate drinks. For the health conscious, Tarla Dalal's *New Indian vegetarian cookbook* (Ebury, 1986) provides recipes for curries and sauces lower in flour, oil and ghee.

The distinctive cuisine of Pakistan is satisfactorily introduced in *Good Housekeeping Pakistani cookery* by Meera Taneja (Ebury, 1985). Though a small book, it offers a wide range of recipes, clearly presented, representing traditional ingredients and authentic dishes.

In the very good "Home book" series, Hsiung Deh-Ta's *Home book of Chinese cookery* (rev. edn, Faber, 1987) has clear recipes aimed at the western user. The writing style is pleasantly informal and there is a helpful introduction. Ken Hom's *Chinese cookery* (BBC, 1985) is the book of the television series. Over 140 recipes from the four main culinary regions of China are effectively set out and well illustrated. The text throughout is clear and explanatory. The same author's *Vegetable and pasta book* (BBC, 1987) broadens the regional scope and offers traditional recipes from China, Japan and South-East Asia. Technique and timing (to avoid over-cooking) are particularly important in

Chinese cooking, and Mei H. Lo and others, *Step by step Chinese cooking* (Century, 1983), has a good basic introduction and recipes arranged by ingredient, each with step-by-step illustrations. There are helpful sections on cooking technique, ingredients and presentation. The philosophy of Chinese food, with gastronomic, medical, social and literary information, is presented alongside more than 100 master recipes in *The Chinese kitchen: a traditional approach to eating* by Yong Yap Cotterell (Weidenfeld & Nicolson, 1986). Dimsum are a feature of Chinese cuisine perhaps best carried out on a large scale in restaurants or big families. However, Margaret Leeming and Man-Hui May Huang's *Dimsum: Chinese light meals, pastries and delicacies* (Macdonald, 1985) provides detailed practical instructions on their preparation, and has a very good glossary.

Japanese cookery is characteristically beautifully prepared and served, and this can be quite daunting to the amateur western cook. Elisabeth Lambert Ortiz, *Japanese cookery* (Collins, 1986), is practical and easy to follow however. There are detailed recipes and help with menu-planning, cutting techniques are fully illustrated, and there is a list of retailers specialising in Japanese foodstuffs. This is an excellent beginner's book, equally appropriate for the more experienced cook, but illustrates the need for patience and enthusiasm. David Scott, *Japanese cooking* (Windward, 1986), perhaps assumes more knowledge and confidence on the part of the user, but is an interesting collection of over 130 recipes for a wide range of dishes including the classics.

There is a literature building up to cover some of the less well-known cuisines of Asia. Anh Thu Stuart, *Vietnamese cooking* (Angus & Robertson, 1986), offers a representative selection of recipes from Northern, Central and Southern Vietnam, ranging from quick and easy meals to the more complex dishes likely to be served at banquets. *A taste of Thailand* by David Scott and Kristiaan Inwood (Rider, 1986) is amusingly written and provides over 200 recipes in a clear and practical style. Alan Davidson, *Seafood of South-East Asia* (Macmillan, 1978) is in the same format as the other seafood books by this author − a catalogue of fish, and recipes that enable the reader to use them effectively and authentically.

Australia

There are surprisingly few books available in this country on Australian cookery, even in the year of the Australian bicentennial celebrations. Traditional recipes, though mostly only of historical interest, are recorded in *The tradition of Australian cooking* by Anne Gollan (Australian National University Press, 1978). The author examines the cooking equipment and methods of the settlers, and traces the development of culinary style in sections headed "The outdoor kitchen"; "The outhouse kitchen"; and "The respectable kitchen". A series of large format paperback cookbooks compiled from recipes published in the *Australian Women's Weekly* is currently available (Sydney: Australian Women's Weekly, n.d.); examples of titles are *The dinner party cookbook; The big book of beautiful biscuits;* and *The barbecue cookbook*. The recipes reflect Australian eating tastes and habits, which, like our own, are modified by the influence of ethnic groups.

A note on Jewish cooking

Jewish cooking is truly international, as it has adapted itself over the centuries to the cuisine of host countries, while never losing its own characteristics. *The Jewish manual,* edited by Chaim Raphael (Sidgwick & Jackson, 1985), is a facsimile of the first Jewish cookbook in English published in 1846. It is subtitled "Practical information in Jewish and modern cookery with a collection of valuable recipes and hints relating to the toilette". There are chapters on soups; sauces and forcemeat; fish; meats and poultry "cooked in various ways"; vegetables, omelettes, fondeaux, croquettes, rissoles, and so on; pastry; sweet dishes, puddings, jellies, creams, charlottes, souffles, gateaux, trifles, custards, cakes, and so on; preserves and bottling; pickling; receipts for invalids. Evelyn Rose, *The complete international Jewish cookbook* (Pan, 1978), provides 650 recipes covering every course and every type of dish or meal, and includes festival foods, with hints on entertaining. *The Jewish festival cookbook* by Gloria Kaufer Greene (Hale, 1988) is also an international cookbook containing over 250 recipes representing Jewish cuisine in countries such as Turkey, Greece, Cuba, Iraq and Algeria. The author relates the stories of the customs and cultures from which the recipes arise.

6

Healthy eating and special diets

Most cookery writers and cookbook compilers would hope that their work did promote healthy and sensible eating, or at least might be offended if accused of encouraging obesity or heart-disease or other food-related problems. However, western society is becoming significantly more interested in the use of natural unprocessed foods, more concerned about the misuse of chemical additives in food manufacture, and more aware of the potential dangers of the high-fat, high-salt, low-fibre diet consumed by much of the population, particularly children. Authors and publishers have responded to, and perhaps stimulated, this concern and awareness with books which aim either to change eating habits for the better, or, more specifically, to prevent or control those diseases and medical conditions which seem to be caused or exacerbated by certain foodstuffs or eating habits. This chapter examines a range of books in each category.

HEALTHY EATING

The NACNE Report – the report of the UK National Advisory Committee on Nutrition Education (HMSO, 1983) – examined the findings of a number of other official government and medical reports on the relationship between eating and health or disease, and came up with clear guidelines on how, and by how much, we need to modify our diets to become healthier. The report is lengthy and technical, and its recommendations will only very slowly infiltrate the nation's diet via food manufacture and marketing, education, and institutional catering. However for concerned and interested individuals Dr Alan Maryon-Davies and Jane Thomas have produced *Diet 2000: at last − a diet you can live with* (Pan, 1984). Based on and stimulated by the NACNE Report, it explains basic nutritional principles, points out the relationships between eating certain types of foods and disease, and outlines a personal eating planner that you can use to assess your own diet. About half the book is then devoted to Diet 2000 recipes and menu suggestions with fat, fibre, sugar and salt ratings. The emphasis is on a balanced diet and encouraging awareness of helpful and harmful foodstuffs without necessarily drastically cutting out all the villains. *A taste of health: the BBC guide to healthy cooking,* edited by Jenny Rogers (BBC, 1985), also takes a very positive approach to eating for health, and describes healthy cooking techniques and equipment. The recipes are provided by nineteen top chefs and cooks and are organised under the conventional headings, but with sections on cheap food, cooking for children, breakfast, and outdoor eating, as topics which also deserve attention. The "healthy diet" recipe books which follow have been included because they are not gimmicky or faddish, but encourage balanced eating based on an awareness of nutritional information. Good Housekeeping, *Good cooking* (Ebury, 1987), provides a "goodness guide" with each recipe (for example the vitamin and fibre content of each), though without information on nutritional requirements at his or her fingertips the user will not necessarily find it easy to plan meals on the basis of this guide. Nutritionist Adelle Davis in *Let's cook it right* (Allen & Unwin, 1970) emphasises, as in all her writing, the importance of cooking food correctly to maintain vitamin and mineral levels, and the recipes exemplify this. An inexpensive and basic guide is Miriam Polunin, *Complete book of diet and health* (Colour Library, 1986), which looks at the place of fats, sugar, salt and fibre in a healthy diet, and at sensible ways of losing weight. The same author has edited *Fast food real food: healthy and enjoyable meals − on the table within ten to thirty minutes* (Thorsons/Newman Turner, 1983). It tells you "how to do" healthy food quickly without relying on convenience foods. Recipes are graded as 10 minute, 20 minute and 30 minute main courses, with sections on desserts, baking, thinking ahead, entertaining and packed meals. Colin Spencer, *Feast for health* (Dorling Kindersley, 1987), deals with everything to be eaten during one week in each season, exemplifying and explaining how to create a balanced diet using fresh foods. Individual food requirements are considered in Karen McNeil's *Book of whole foods* (Hale, 1986) with advice on diets geared to age, sex, metabolic rate and amount of physical activity. Information on the nutritional value and the cooking of natural foods is supplied along with fifty original recipes.

High-fibre, low-fat, low-sugar and low-sodium cooking

A range of recipes is provided in *Cook yourself a favour: 350 recipes to help you help yourself to better health* by S. Gibson *et al* (Thorsons, 1986). Wheat-free, dairy-free and egg-free diets can also be put together from this book. Audrey Eyton, *The F-Plan* (Penguin, 1982), has achieved considerable fame, and is a guide and recipe book advocating a high-fibre diet as a slimming method, though it is useful for anyone needing a high-fibre diet. Alison Leach and Jane Lewis, *High fibre cookery* (Octopus, 1986), aims to extend the use of high-fibre ingredients in standard cooking to improve digestion and general health. Low-fat recipes may be a medical requirement for some people, or simply a matter of personal choice. Anny Mauder's *New low fat recipes* (Foulsham, 1986) have a very low fat content, taking a number of medical conditions into account. Scott Ewing, *The Jack Sprat cookbook: delicious low-fat food* (Grafton, 1986), contains 150 recipes, some new, some low-fat versions of well-known dishes. *Not naughty but nice* by Liza Goddard and Ann Baldwin (Ward Lock, 1987) provides sugar- and milk-free recipes for sauces; soufflés; main courses; puddings; baking and preserves. Familiar recipes are translated into wholefood and low-sugar versions in Jacqui Hine, *Here's Health guide to low-sugar cooking* (Thorsons, 1987). There are also recipes for weaning babies. Friends of the Earth have a booklet, *Sweet and low − in sugar* (n.d.), with recipes for snacks, cakes, puddings, drinks and assorted other eatables using little or no sugar. It is worth writing for a publication list, to Friends of the Earth, 54 Allison Street, Birmingham.

Wholefoods and health foods

Many of the cookery books mentioned in the Healthy eating, Vegetarian, Special diet and more general sections of this work advise or assume the use of wholefoods, which at its most precise means

PUDDINGS

Apple, Soya & Almond Pudding

675 g (1½ lb) cooking apples,
finely chopped
150 ml (¼ pt) boiling water
100 g (4 oz) butter
50 ml (2 fl oz) honey
1 egg, beaten
juice and grated rind of 1 lemon
75 g (3 oz) ground almonds
25 g (1 oz) soya flour
¼ tsp vanilla essence
2.5 ml (½ tsp) baking powder (use
appropriate baking powder for
recipe, see p. 133)

Preparation 15 minutes
Cooking 30-40 minutes
Serves 4
ⒼⒻ

**You can substitute fresh plums or peaches for the apples, when
they are in season.**

1 Heat the oven to 180°C (350°F/Gas 4).

2 Put the apples into a medium-sized saucepan, add the water and
stew gently for 5 minutes.

3 In a bowl, cream together the butter and honey. Add the egg to
the creamed mixture and mix well.

4 Add the lemon juice and rind.

5 Add the almonds, soya flour, vanilla essence and baking powder
and beat together until you have a smooth mixture.

6 Put the apples in an ovenproof dish.

7 Spread the cake mixture over the top and bake for 30-40 minutes
or until golden brown on top.

Serve immediately with yogurt or cream.

Figure 6.1   Wholefood recipes attractively produced

90

Apricot & Orange Sago Cream

225 g (8 oz) dried apricots, soaked
   for 12 hours or overnight
juice and grated rind of 1 orange
570 ml (1 pt) milk
100 g (4 oz) sago
2 eggs, separated

**Preparation 20 minutes (allow 12 hours
for soaking the apricots)**
Cooking 20 minutes
Chilling 2 hours minimum
Serves 4
(GF)

You will need a blender for this recipe.

1 Drain the apricots and reserve 4 for decoration. Purée the rest, together with the orange juice, in a blender and set aside.

2 Put the milk, sago and orange rind in a medium-sized saucepan and simmer gently for 15 minutes or until the sago is cooked. Stir occasionally to prevent sticking.

3 Add the egg yolks and heat gently for a further 5 minutes.

4 Remove from the heat and stir in the puréed apricots. Cool.

5 Whip the egg whites stiffly and fold into the cooled sago mixture.

6 Pour into 4 individual dishes and chill in the refrigerator for at least 2 hours before serving. Decorate with the reserved apricots.

Baked Apples

6 large cooking apples, cored

Stuffing
175 g (6 oz) mixed dried fruit,
   finely chopped
30 ml (2 tbsp) honey or apple juice
   concentrate (see p. 51)
5 ml (1 tsp) mixed spice
2.5 ml (½ tsp) ground cloves
75 g (3 oz) regular oats

Preparation 10 minutes
Cooking 30 minutes
Serves 6
(V)

The dried fruit needs to be chopped very finely, to ensure thorough cooking.

1 Heat the oven to 220°C (425°F/Gas 7).

2 Place the apples on a greased baking tray.

3 Make the stuffing: mix together the mixed dried fruit, honey, mixed spice, cloves and oats.

4 Using a teaspoon, fill the centres of the apples with the stuffing.

5 Bake in the oven for 30 minutes or until the apples are soft.

Serve warm with whipped cream, yogurt or custard.

Baked Bananas with Yogurt Sauce

15 ml (1 tbsp) honey
75 g (3 oz) butter
5 ml (1 tsp) mixed spice
6 bananas

Sauce
425 ml (¾ pt) Greek-style yogurt
75 ml (3 fl oz) single cream
¼ tsp ground cardamom
5 ml (1 tsp) grated nutmeg
15 ml (1 tbsp) honey
juice and grated rind of 1 orange or
   1 lemon

Preparation 10 minutes
Cooking 20 minutes
Serves 6
(GF)

1 Heat the oven to 180°C (350°F/Gas 4).

2 Gently melt the honey and butter in a small saucepan and add the mixed spice.

3 Coat the bananas in the mixture and place on an oiled baking tray.

4 Bake for 20 minutes or until the bananas are soft.

5 Meanwhile, make the yogurt sauce: mix all the sauce ingredients together. Pour over the hot bananas and serve immediately.

Source: Rachel Haigh, *The Neal's Yard Bakery wholefood cookbook* (Dorling Kindersley, 1986), pp. 120–1. Reproduced by kind permission of Dorling Kindersley Publishers Ltd.

organically grown produce without the use of supplementary chemicals at any stage of its growth or production. More broadly it refers to the use of fresh, unprocessed and even unfrozen foods in cooking and meal preparation. In both cases there is an emphasis on vegetables, pulses, grains and fruit, with minimal or no meat. "Health foods" are the foods found on the shelves of health food shops – and can include wholefood items such as organically produced pulses, cereals and dried fruits, processed or manufactured foods such as meat substitutes and caffeine-free drinks, and canned goods such as meat-free stews, but include also many proprietary food supplements in tablet or liquid form which, according to many nutritionists, are unnecessary if a balanced diet is followed.

Some recipe books emphasise the use of wholefoods. *The wholefood book* by George Seddon and Jackie Burrow (Mitchell Beazley, 1978) offers nutritional information and recipes for "whole ingredients that have nothing lost and nothing added". *The Neal's Yard Bakery wholefood cookbook* by Rachel Haigh (Dorling Kindersley, 1986; paperback edn, 1988) contains, among others, many recipes for dishes served in the restaurant run by the Neal's Yard Bakery Cooperative. It is packed with nutritional information and recommends the use of organic produce where possible. Some of the ingredients used in the recipes, such as the seaweeds, need to be obtained from specialised wholefood or health food shops. The book is attractively illustrated with photographic "aerial views" of ingredients and finished dishes. There are recipes for breakfasts, soups, starters, salads, main courses, puddings, cakes, pastries, biscuits and scones, and breads (Figure 6.1).

Health foods are given separate treatment in Evelyn Findlater's *Off the shelf: the healthfood shopper's brandname cookbook* (Century, 1987). Over 200 recipes for soups, salads, vegetable and pasta dishes, main meals, baking and desserts, incorporate branded health food products.

VEGETARIAN COOKING

Vegetarian diets avoid the use of meat, game, poultry and fish – in other words the consumption of living creatures; cookery writers are now also identifying "demi-vegetarians", those who confine themselves to white meats such as chicken and fish.

Rose Elliott is a long-established vegetarian cookery writer, and her *Complete vegetarian cookbook* (Collins, 1985) is a substantial work which pulls together over 1000 recipes from her many Fontana paperbacks published between 1967 and 1985. It is a clear, basic and inexpensive work. Another useful and inexpensive work is *The home book of vegetarian cookery* (Faber, 1979), first published in 1964 and written by N. B. and R. B. Highton who started the famous Vega restaurant in London. It contains practical recipes covering all branches of vegetarian cookery. Many national cuisines have a high proportion of vegetarian dishes, and *The international vegetarian: 200 delicious recipes from three continents* by David Scott and Jack Santa Maria (Rider, 1986) represents Greece, Turkey, the Middle East, Japan, India, China, Britain and the Mediterranean, though using readily available ingredients. Diana Troy, *The Covent Garden cookery book* (Sidgwick & Jackson, 1987), concentrates on British vegetarian cookery going back to the medieval use of grains and pulses, and stresses the use of flavourings to avoid blandness. Gourmet cooking is the subject of Susanna Tee's *Good Housekeeping vegetarian gourmet* (Ebury Press, 1986) with over 250 recipes in the usual clear Good Housekeeping style; and of Colin Spencer's *The new vegetarian: the ultimate guide to gourmet cooking and healthy living* (Elm Tree, 1986). In this work, as well as recipes there is information on diet and menu-planning; menus for festive cooking contributed by guest authors; and advice on alternatives to salt, sugar and fat. Menu-planning is the essence of *Vegetarian meals* (Octopus, 1986) in the Menu Masters series, and describes 15 menus for a range of occasions, each with a detailed work schedule. At the other end of the time scale is David Scott, *The 30 minute vegetarian: over 200 fast and easy recipes for the healthy cook in a hurry* (Century, 1986). The title speaks for itself. Recipes are arranged in the usual categories. Seasonal produce is particularly significant in vegetarian cooking, and Janet Hunt's *365 plus one vegetarian main meals* (Thorsons, 1987) provides a recipe for every day of the year (plus one!) divided into the four seasons to facilitate the use of seasonal produce. Summer and outdoor eating is the theme of Felicity Jackson's *Vegetarian barbecue and summer cooking* (Windward, 1987). Barbecue cooking is normally meat-based, but here ideas are given for vegetarian foods which can be cooked on a barbecue, and for summer meals and picnics. Vegetarian cooking for one is covered by Marlis Weber, *The single vegetarian* (Thorsons, 1987), which gives a range of quick and economical recipes. The vegetarian on the move is catered for in Andrew Sanger's *Vegetarian traveller* (Thorsons, 1987), a country-by-country guide to eating out and self-catering without meat or fish in Europe and the Mediterranean. Kitty Campion, *The vegetarian encyclopaedia: an A – Z of nutrition and well-being* (Century, 1986), is a useful reference work listing ingredients for a complete vegetarian diet arranged alphabetically, and giving food values and recipe ideas. Colin Spencer and Tom Sanders, *The vegetarians' healthy diet book* (Martin Dunitz, 1986), explains how to achieve a balanced diet and avoid vitamin deficiency; it provides 150 recipes balancing protein, fat and carbohydrate. For those vegetarians who also need a high protein diet, Frances Moore Lappé, *Diet for a small planet* (Ballantine, 1975), provides hundreds of complementary protein dishes for meatless high protein dishes.

VEGAN COOKING

Vegans eat no meat, eggs or dairy produce for reasons of economy, health, or concern about the abuse of livestock at all stages of food production. The Vegan Society publishes leaflets, pamphlets and books explaining the vegan philosophy and providing recipes and details of commercially available alternatives to dairy produce. Eva Batt, *Vegan cookery* (new edn, Thorsons, 1985), was originally published as *What's cooking* (1974) and is produced in cooperation with the Vegan Society. It is an informative book with a full range of recipes, clearly set out. The same author has written *What else is cooking? Further adventures in cooking with compassion* (Vegan Society, 1983). This is a substantial work with recipes for soups, salads, salad dressings, savoury dishes, stuffings, gravies and sauces, vegetable dishes, desserts and sweets, bread, cakes, biscuits, pastries, sweets, preserves, and alternatives to dairy foods. Leah Leneman in *Vegan cooking: the compassionate way of eating* (Thorsons, 1982) wishes to emphasise the variety of foods and dishes available to vegans, and has produced a very thorough work which starts with recipes for milk, cream, ice-cream, cheese and yoghurt substitutes; and then arranges recipes under headings tofu; soups; salads and snacks; cereals and pasta; pulse dishes; vegetable- and nut-based dishes; cakes; and desserts. There is also a section of recipes using prepared health-food products. Recipes are clearly set out step-by-step.

There is a short (40 page) introductory pamphlet by Sandra Williams and Joy Scott called *Easy vegan cooking* (Old Hammond Press, 1985) with a very basic range of recipes for the novice. *The vegan cookbook* by Alan Wakeman and Gordon Baskerville (Faber, 1986) is a collection of over 200 imaginative recipes produced in an inexpensive and basic format.

NEARLY VEGETARIAN COOKING

For those who want a healthier diet avoiding fatty high-cholesterol meats but do not wish to commit themselves fully to vegetarianism, there are books available offering a new combination of recipes. David Scott's *The demiveg cookbook* (Bloomsbury, 1987) is based on chicken, fish and vegetables; Richard Cawley, *Not quite vegetarian* (Macdonald, 1986), avoids red meat but uses chicken and fish in combination with other fresh ingredients; and Jean Conil, *Cuisine fraîcheur* (Aurum Press, 1987), provides recipes based on raw vegetables and fruit with lightly cooked eggs, beans, poultry and fish to supply protein.

MACROBIOTIC COOKING

A macrobiotic diet is a vegetarian wholefood diet containing a critical balance of acids and alkalis. A thorough and up to date cookbook is Keith Michell, *Practically macrobiotic: ingredients, preparation and cooking of more than 200 delicious macrobiotic recipes* (Thorsons, 1987). It describes the philosophy of the diet; alphabetically lists macrobiotic ingredients; and is an attractively produced and easy to use work.

WEIGHT-LOSS DIETS

Though many of the "healthy eating" diets used in conjunction with exercise should encourage weight loss, there will probably always be a demand for slimming diets from those who wish to slim for cosmetic or psychological benefits rather than as a medical requirement. There are many books whose stated purpose is to help the reader lose weight, and those examined here are not fad diets — bananas only, or grapefruit with everything — but those advocating balanced eating patterns for good general health. The slimming organisations have produced helpful guides. *The make it simple! cookbook* by Ann Page-Wood (New English Library, 1987) is a Weight Watchers' guide to simple meals with step-by-step instructions. More complex meals are covered in the same organisation's *Cooking around the world with Weight Watchers* (New English Library, 1986) which gives calorie-reduced versions of gourmet recipes. *Slimming* magazine has produced *Slimming: the complete guide* (rev. edn, Collins, 1987) which outlines new diets and incorporates new nutritional information, particularly on the importance of fibre. A book to give round-the-year support to the slimmer is Richard Williams, *Diet for life* (Crowood, 1986), a 52 week programme which divides the year into four 12 week sessions — each based on a theme — aiming at weight reduction and the general re-education of eating habits. In the gift book category for the slimmer is *The Champneys cookbook* by Mark Hickman and Danielle Truman (Guinness Books, 1987). Champneys is a health spa, and the book gives low-calorie recipes for English and international cuisine served there. There is fat and fibre information with each recipe and the step-by-step presentation is clear and helpful. Audrey Eyton, *The F-plan* (Penguin, 1982), is essentially a slimming diet based on a high fibre intake for the health of the digestive tract, and to satisfy the need for bulk while reducing calorie intake. All the above books cover the full range of recipes, but there are books available that specialise in types of dish — for example, *Fresh ways with desserts* (Time-Life, 1987) contains 120 recipes for desserts averaging only 175 calories per portion.

DIETS FOR MEDICAL CONDITIONS

Certain diseases and medical conditions, particularly those of the digestive tract, have long been treated by the use of specific diets. However in the last ten years there has been a massive increase in public interest in how nutrition relates to diseases of the western world, so that more and more books are being written to encourage the layman to manage his or her own mild and chronic conditions using nutritional methods. An as yet incomplete medical text has been edited and rewritten for the layman, and is perhaps one of the most thorough guides to nutrition and illness. It is *Nutritional medicine: the drug-free guide to better family health* by Dr Stephen Davies and Dr Alan Stewart (Pan Books, 1987). It is not a recipe book but gives detailed information on foods to avoid and foods to use for specific conditions. There is an introduction explaining nutritional principles and the problems associated with western diets. There are then substantial sections on each of the following: Nutrients and anti-nutrients; Allergies; The nutritional management of some diseases and common ailments (these include cancer, bone and joint conditions, obesity, infections, migraine, and many others). Appendices cover Living healthily; Nutritional deficiencies and supplements; Exclusion diets and food lists; Information sources (mostly self-help groups and patient support groups for the layman). There are case histories throughout. A good outline of the development of current dietary thinking and the implications for the treatment of medical problems is Barbara Griggs, *The food factor: an account of the nutrition revolution* (Viking, 1986). Specifically on foodstuffs is Carol A. Rinzler, *Food facts* (Bloomsbury, 1987), a handbook in alphabetical order of foods, giving the nutritional profile for each (based on information supplied in government publications; see Chapter 2, p. 29), recommended daily amounts; and information on storage, preparation, the effects of processing, medical uses and benefits, possible adverse effects, and food/drug interactions. It is a useful reference tool for anyone suffering from an allergy or with constant drug requirements, or simply interested in modifying their own diet for better general health.

There are a number of books in this field containing recipes. Celia Wright, *The Wright diet* (Piatkus, 1986), is written in a slightly tub-thumping way ("The Wright Diet is the healthiest diet in the world") but the dietary principles are sound and recognise that individual nutritional needs vary. The author explains the diet, looks at a range of ailments and medical problems and the dietary requirements for each, and provides a selection of recipes. Foods are classified into those that can be eaten freely, those that should be limited, and those that should be totally excluded except on special occasions. The recipes reflect these classifications, and it is then up to the reader to devise appropriate menus from the recipes and other nutritional information in the book. Bee Nilson, *Cooking for special diets* (2nd edn, Penguin, 1971), explains a number of medical conditions and diets under headings General diets;

Diseases of the digestive system; Diseases of the liver, gall bladder and bile duct; Diabetes; Overweight; Diseases of the cardio-vascular or circulatory system; Diseases of the kidneys and urinary tract; Undernutrition; Fevers and infections; Anaemia; Gout; Diseases of childhood; Diet in old age. There are then nearly 600 recipes arranged under fairly standard headings, but helpfully each section on diseases gives sample menus.

Some books focus on diets for specific illnesses and conditions, and some examples of these are examined below.

Cancer

The Bristol Diet: a get well and stay well eating plan by Dr Alec Forbes (Century Arrow, 1986) is based on the diet used to treat patients at the Bristol Cancer Help Centre, though it was originally devised to develop positive eating habits in anyone in order to prevent disease. The emphasis is on vegetables (often raw for high vitamin and mineral levels) and whole grains, avoiding sugar, salt and chemical additives — very close to a vegan diet in fact. Half the book is devoted to the chemistry of food and nutritional information related to disease, and half to recipes and menus. A fuller collection of recipes is available in *The Bristol recipe book* by Sadhya Rippon (Century, 1987).

Pre-menstrual tension

Dietary advice on PMT is given in Celia Wright's book *The Wright Diet* (above), but more detailed methods are given in Maryon Stewart's *Beat PMT through diet* (Ebury Press, 1987), a programme developed by the PMT Advisory Service. The book identifies four main types of PMT, and a questionnaire enables the sufferer to identify which of these she suffers from. She is then required to make simple dietary changes to help relieve the symptoms. A selection of recipes is provided.

Diabetes

The complete diabetic cookbook by Joyce Daly Margie and Dr P. J. Palumbo (Grafton, 1987) describes itself as "the diabetic cookbook that comprehensively covers the medical problem and its treatment through diet". It provides background information on the condition, and on exercise, nutrition and meal planning, with a full collection of recipes each with a food analysis. Jill Metcalfe, *Cooking the new diabetic way: the high fibre calorie-conscious cookbook* (Ward Lock, 1987) is an updated edition of a book originally published in 1983. The author is a dietitian at the British Diabetic Association and she uses the Association's latest dietary findings in the recipes. Barbara Davidson's *New diabetic cookbook* (Octopus, 1986) places emphasis on a planned daily intake of high-fibre foods that are low in fat and sugar-free. High-fibre foods are also the focus of over 250 recipes in *The diabetic high fibre cookbook* by Mary Jane Finsand (Blandford, 1986). Diabetics with a sweet tooth are catered for by Jane Suthering in *Diabetic delights: cakes, biscuits and desserts* (Martin Dunitz, 1986), which contains 150 calorie-counted recipes each with a statement of nutritional values. There is also Elbie Lebrecht's *Sugar-free cakes and biscuits: recipes for diabetics and dieters* (Faber, 1985).

Diabetic children are specifically catered for in *The diabetic kids' cookbook* by Jane Rossiter and Rosemary Seddon (Macdonald Optima, 1987). Essential information on nutrition and dietary principles is provided in full, but the book differs from other diabetic cookery books in its collection of recipes for dishes likely to attract children, and there is a small section on goodies that children can cook for themselves.

Allergies

Food allergies are sometimes dramatic and obvious, such as developing a rash or swelling after eating specific foods like strawberries or shellfish, and these are relatively easily dealt with. Other allergies may result in chronic but less clear-cut symptoms, and may be caused by a complex of foods so that the allergy is difficult to identify and treat. Tests, usually using elimination or exclusion diets, are the starting point, and there are books available that offer guidance. Elizabeth Workman, Dr John Hunter and Dr Virginia Alun Jones explain the Addenbrooke's Hospital step-by-step exclusion diet plan in *The allergy diet: how to overcome your food intolerance* (Martin Dunitz, 1984). There is general information on diet and allergies, advice on how to start and monitor the exclusion diet, and sample menus. An attractive collection of 150 recipes is provided and covers breakfasts, drinks, starters and soups, salads and vegetables, vegetarian dishes, snacks, fish, meat, poultry and game, stocks, batters, sauces, dressings, bakery, fruit and puddings. *The allergy cookbook* by Andrew Cant and Danila Armstrong (Octopus, 1986) also explains how to plan and work an exclusion diet, and then how to re-plan the daily diet avoiding foods to which there is an allergenic response.

Some of the most common allergies are caused by dairy products, eggs and certain grains, and it is possible to devise a diet without using them. Billie Little's *Recipes for allergics* (Bantam, 1983) gives recipes for corn-, egg-, milk- and wheat-free diets and combinations of those, plus general dietary information. The lists of suppliers and literature are American, but it is a useful recipe book. *The allergy cookbook: tasty nutritious cooking without wheat, corn, milk or eggs* by Ruth Shattuck (Century, 1985) has an informative introduction and gives over 200 recipes for breads; cakes, biscuits, flans; desserts; meatless meals; meat and fish dishes; and soups, avoiding the common allergens. Hilda Cherry Hills, *Good food: grain-free milk-free* (Roberts, 1978), was written specifically with schizophrenia patients in mind and gives a thorough listing of forbidden and acceptable foods and drinks and a full range of recipes. There is guidance on eating out, and sources of product supply.

Specifically gluten-free diets are required by sufferers from Coeliac disease and dermatitis herpetiformis. The classic work is Hilda Cherry Hills, *Good food gluten-free* (Roberts, 1973), which gives a sound outline of the nutritional principles involved, and hundreds of recipes. Rita Greer's *Gluten-free cooking* (2nd rev. edn, Thorsons, 1983) has recipes arranged by type of dish (including "festival food"), and notes on "coping generally" and shopping. *The gluten-free diet book* by Dr Peter Rawcliffe and Ruth Rolph (Martin Dunitz, 1985) explains conditions such as Coeliac disease and dermatitis herpetiformis, describes the diet and how to cope with it, and gives a good collection of recipes.

Renal failure

Kidney patients need a balanced diet that their kidneys can cope with, and this is fully explained in *Enjoying food on a renal diet,* edited by Marianne Vennegoor (King's Fund Publishing Office, 1982). There is a good collection of recipes allowing a near-normal diet, with a food analysis of each one so that recipes can be modified to suit individual needs. The book is compiled by the Renal Group of the British Dietetic Association.

Arthritis

With so much uncertainty surrounding some of the drug treatments for arthritis combined with what seems to be substantial evidence that care with diet can alleviate the pain, stiffness and swelling associated with the condition, it is natural that dietary treatments should have become popular. A reliable work is the *Curing arthritis cookbook* by Margaret Hills (Sheldon Press, 1987), a book of acid-free and relatively simple recipes. Mary Laver and Margaret Smith, *Diet for life: a cookbook for arthritics* (Pan, 1981), is based on the Dong diet developed in America by Dr Collin Dong, himself an arthritis sufferer. This inexpensive paperback outlines the principles of the diet and provides calorie charts and a wide range of recipes backed up by nutritional information.

Feeding babies and children

Cookery books in this section fall mainly into two categories — those aimed at "normal" children and those providing dietary information for allergic and other problem eaters. In the first category the emphasis is on a varied but healthy diet. On the basis that a baby's health and nutritional needs are affected before as well as after conception, Foresight, the Association for the Promotion of Pre-conceptual care, emphasises the need for a wholesome diet at all stages of life. *The Foresight wholefoods cookbook — for building healthy families* by Norman and Ruth Jervis (Roberts, 1984) offers 150 pages of varied and interesting wholefood recipes as well as informative chapters on infant feeding; allergy; hyperactivity and metal toxicity; overweight; and nutrition. *Growing up with good food,* edited by Catherine Lewis (Unwin, 1982), was first published in 1978 by the National Childbirth Trust. Now revised and expanded, it is packed with information, ideas and recipes for feeding babies in their first year; family meals; vegetarian meals; cakes, biscuits and preserves; children's parties and birthday cakes; and cooking with children [sic]. Gail Duff, *Good food — healthy children* (Conran Octopus, 1986), has sections on nutritional requirements and diet at each stage of a child's development, and then

GRAIN FREE DUMPLINGS

Grain Free   Gluten Free   Milk Free

Imperial (Metric)

1 oz (30g) margarine (milk free)
2 free range eggs
1 oz (30g) chickpea flour
1 oz (30g) potato flour
1 oz (30g) soya flour°
1 heaped teaspoon baking powder
(grain free)
pinch of sea salt and freshly ground
pepper
hot stew, soup or broth

American

2½ tablespoons margarine (milk
free)
2 free range eggs
1½ tablespoons garbanzo bean flour
1½ tablespoons potato flour
¼ cup soy flour
1 heaped teaspoon baking powder
(grain free)
pinch of sea salt and freshly ground
pepper
hot stew, soup or broth

1. Soften the margarine and beat it with eggs until creamy.

2. Gradually stir in flours that have been mixed together well. Add nutmeg, salt and pepper. Make sure the mixture is well blended. It should be fairly stiff.

3. Drop teaspoons of mixture into simmering stew, soup or broth. Cook for 10 minutes and serve.

Note: Other flours may be substituted for the above (see page 235).

SCRAMBLED EGG WITH VEGETABLES

Add vegetables of choice — sweetcorn, runner beans, beansprouts and mushrooms, etc. to egg mixture and cook as usual. Serve on bread and butter, toast and/or with salad greens, e.g. lettuce, watercress.

Figure 6.2   Non-allergenic food for problematic children

LEMON CHICKEN

Grain Free   Gluten Free   Milk Free   Egg Free

Imperial (Metric)

1 clove garlic, skinned and crushed
3 tablespoons sunflower oil
sea salt and freshly ground pepper to
taste
juice of 2 lemons
1 onion, skinned and grated
4 chicken portions, skinned

American

1 clove garlic, skinned and crushed
3 tablespoons sunflower oil
sea salt and freshly ground pepper to
taste
juice of 2 lemons
1 onion, skinned and grated
4 chicken portions, skinned

1. Mix garlic, oil, seasoning, lemon juice and grated onion together in a bowl.

2. Wash and dry chicken pieces. Place them in a shallow dish and pour over the marinade. Leave to marinate for 1-2 hours.

3. Arrange the chicken pieces in the grill (broiler) pan and pour over the marinade. Grill, basting frequently, under medium heat for 30-40 minutes, or until the chicken is cooked through. Serve with any remaining juices.

VEGETABLE AND POTATO PIE

Put layers of any vegetables, such as marrow (summer squash), courgettes (zucchini), cooked mashed swede (rutabaga) or parsnips, thin slices of onion. Add a little vegetable stock with yeast extract and cover with mashed potato and grated cheese. Serve with a green vegetable or salad.

Source: Janet Ash and Dulcie Roberts, *Happiness is junk-free food* (Thorsons, 1986), pp. 92–3. Reproduced by kind permission of Thorsons Publishing Group.

recipes for imaginative foods avoiding too much sugar and fat; there is a large section on "portable food". Joanna Pay, *Cooking for kids the healthy way: wholesome recipes with child appeal* (Dunitz, 1986), has an informative introduction on overweight children, problem eaters, and so on, and is an excellent collection of recipes. The author is a qualified dietitian and nutritionist. Rosamond Richardson, *Vegetarian cooking for children* (Piatkus, 1986), is a collection of recipes for the family but which children should enjoy; many of the dishes can be prepared by children.

Hyperactivity and other allergies

Hyperactivity in children seems to be closely related to diet, and *The hyperactive child* by Belinda Barnes and Irene Colquhoun (Thorsons, 1984) offers self-help approaches to coping with the problem. There is a chapter on nutrition, recipes, and a substantial appendix describing special diets including the Feingold Food Programme. *Happiness is junk-free food* by Janet Ash and Dulcie Roberts (Thorsons, 1986) is subtitled "Fight hyperactivity and other food allergies with quick and easy healthy meals for all the family". Written to "help mothers of problematic children" (Figure 6.2) it provides recipes concentrating on fresh unprocessed foods, and avoiding the "junk" which contains chemical additives, and refined sugars and flours. It is a key work, full of common sense and manageable objectives. Proceeds on the sale of the book go to the Hyperactive Children's Support Group. Pauline Moore's *New milk-free, egg-free recipes for children* (Foulsham, 1986) provides recipes for pancakes, hot chocolate, biscuits, cakes and puddings.

DIETS FOR OLDER PEOPLE

Older people often lose interest in food, sometimes for physical reasons, sometimes because if they live alone it is more of an effort to shop and cook for one, especially as packaging in supermarkets — often the nearest and cheapest food shop — is not geared to the requirements of single people and reduced appetites. Books that might bolster flagging enthusiasm are Louise Davies, *Easy cooking for one or two* (Penguin, 1972) and *More easy cooking for one or two* (Penguin, 1979). Both provide a collection of simple and nutritious recipes aimed at the elderly and printed in large type for easier use, and are based on the author's work in geriatric nutrition. *Cooking in retirement* by Dan and Molly Lees (Croom Helm, 1987) offers advice on saving time, energy and money, effective shopping for one or two, and cooking equipment; and provides recipes for easy meals. *Enjoy cooking for one* by A. Taveren and L. Sweeney (Glasgow: Queen's College, 1979) gives advice on diet, menu-planning and shopping, with recipes suitable for people living alone – particularly the elderly. Age Concern in association with Kerrygold have produced *One plus one: simple nourishing recipes for one and two* (Mitcham: Age Concern, 1981).

DIETS FOR ATHLETES

A recent helpful work using up to date nutritional information is *Food for action* (Pelham, 1987). It offers guidelines for a healthy diet and special regimes to gain, restrict or maintain weight, and describes the effects of drug-taking among athletes. There seem to be few recipe books available specifically about diets for athletes; the emphasis is on nutritional principles. *Food for sport: a handbook of sports nutrition* by Peter Berry Ottaway and Kevin Hargin (Resource Publications Basic Skills Unit, 1985) examines, in a fairly technical way, topics such as energy nutrients, energy requirements, the place of vitamins, minerals and fluids in the athlete's diet, and meal planning. Some sample recipes are provided as an appendix. It is a thorough work, though quite short, which should enable the user to develop an appropriate dietary regime for his or her needs.

Index